Kevin Reddick offers us, through transparent penmanship, *The Lazarus Connection,* which provides an in-depth look at the resurrection power and promise of our Lord and Savior Jesus Christ. This book connects the many intersections, highways, and byways that lead to God's ultimate desire for every Christian believer—to be reconciled with Him and His predestined plan for their lives. Lazarus was dead, buried, and perhaps dismissed because at death, in man's limited scope, there's no chance of being resurrected. His sisters witnessed the death; friends and the community knew of his demise—but God. . . .

Even at the point of death, God's perfect will for every Christian shall be done. Like Lazarus, God is calling you to come forth from confusion, fear, self-destruction, pain, opinions of others, substance abuse, poverty, hopelessness, conflicting spiritual ideologies, and everything that attempts to hold you captive and in bondage. *The Lazarus Connection* addresses the many complexities and challenges of life, while still resting in the assurance of God's ability to resurrect and restore any person or situation that has been identified and declared dead. "Lazarus, come forth!"

—Bishop Stephen A. Davis, Pastor,
New Birth Missionary Baptist Church, Lithonia, Georgia

Elder Kevin Reddick is a product of redemption and transformation. There are not many individuals who would tell an open story to a closed public—but he has shown through this book that God and persistence are the keys to excelling in a world of complicated ideas. Elder, I am proud of your growth and dedication to God. I am praying for many blessings.

—Pastor Omar Jahwar, Pastor, Kingdom Restoration Church,
Dallas, Texas, and Founder and Director, Urban Specialists,
Dallas, Texas

The Lazarus Connection

The Lazarus Connection

Kevin Reddick

REDEMPTION
PRESS

ISBN 13: 978-1-68314-313-0
978-1-68314-314-7 (ePub)
978-1-68314-315-4 (Mobi)

Library of Congress Catalog Card Number: 2017939736

Dedication

THIS BOOK IS dedicated to all of the individuals who have been pronounced dead by family and friends. To those who feel and believe that their dreams, desires, and purpose are dead due to various types of addictions and strongholds in their lives. And to those who are at this moment out of the grave, but still wrapped in grave clothes.

Table of Contents

Acknowledgments

TO MY WIFE, Bonita, who sowed time, pain, prayer, faith, love, and tears into my life while holding fast to the promises of God. I love you and thank you for loving me.

To my sons, Mustafa and Malcolm. May my journey be used to guide and lead you to continue God's work in our bloodline. May your growth from faith to faith and glory to glory flow through your children's children's children.

To my spiritual father and mother, Apostle Eddie L. Long and First Lady Vanessa Long. I would have to write another book to express all that you have done for and mean to me. Thank you for standing and being who you are. I owe a great deal of my living in Christ to you. I love you both very much.

To my Pastor, Bishop Stephen A. Davis and his wife, First Lady Darlene Davis, New Birth Missionary Baptist Church, Stonecrest, Georgia. Thank you for activating me into a higher level of service to God and being a great example of a man submitted to God and his spiritual father.

I also want to thank Pastor Paula White and Church Without Walls, Pastor Rod Parsley and World Harvest Church, and Dr. Creflo Dollar and World Changers Church. The late Dr. Myles Monroe and Bahamas Faith Ministries International, and Bishop J.D. Jakes and The Potter's House Church.

To Dr. Kenneth and Candy Harper and Jerry and Felicia Wilson, for allowing the love and presence of their beautiful daughters to remove some of the sting of loss of my own. I cannot express what your kindness has meant to my wife and me. Thank you.

A special thanks to all of my dear friends and associates who, for whatever reason, made room in their hearts to love, encourage, support, cover, speak into, and pray for me.

To my brothers of Manhood 712. Thank you for sharpening me in my dull areas and allowing me the honor to be used by God to help sharpen and shape you to be the swords of the Spirit God intends us to be.

Chapter 1

Lazarus and I

I BELIEVE IT would be inappropriate for me to presume that everyone who picks up this book knows who Lazarus is and to which Lazarus I am referring. Since I would consider this foundational, allow me to present this Lazarus to you.

> Now a certain man was sick, Lazarus of Bethany, the town of Mary and her sister Martha. It was that Mary who anointed the Lord with fragrant oil and wiped His feet with her hair, whose brother Lazarus was sick. Therefore the sisters sent to Him, saying, "Lord, behold, he whom You love is sick." When Jesus heard that, He said, "This sickness is not unto death, but for the glory of God, that the Son of God may be glorified through it." Now Jesus loved Martha and her sister and Lazarus. So when He heard that he was sick, He stayed two more days in the place where He was. Then after this He said to the disciples, "Let us go to Judea again. . . . "

> He said to them, "Our friend Lazarus sleeps, but I go that I may wake him up." Then His disciples said, "Lord, if he sleeps he will get well." However, Jesus spoke of his death, but they thought that He was

speaking about taking rest in sleep. Then Jesus said to them plainly, "Lazarus is dead. And I am glad for your sakes that I was not there, that you may believe. Nevertheless, let us go to him."

So when Jesus came, He found that Lazarus had already been in the tomb four days. Bethany was near Jerusalem, about two miles away. Many of the Jews had joined the women around Martha and Mary to comfort them concerning their brother.

Martha, as soon as she heard that Jesus was coming, went and met Him, but Mary was sitting in the house. Now Martha said to Jesus, "Lord, if You had been here, my brother would not have died. But even now I know that whatever You ask of God, God will give You."

Jesus said to her, "Your brother will rise again."

Martha said to Him, I know that he will rise again in the resurrection at the last day."

Jesus said to her, "I am the resurrection and the life. He who believes in Me, though he may die, he shall live. And whoever lives and believes in Me shall never die. Do you believe this?"

She said to Him, "Yes, Lord, I believe that You are the Christ, the Son of God, who is come into the world." And when she had said these things, she went her way and secretly called Mary her sister, saying, "The Teacher has come and is calling for you." As soon as she heard that, she arose quickly and came to Him. Now Jesus had not yet come into the town, but was in the place where Martha met Him. Then the Jews who were with her in the house, and comforting her, when they saw that Mary rose up quickly and went out, followed her, saying, "She is going to the tomb to weep there." Then, when Mary came where Jesus was, and saw Him, she fell down at His feet, saying to Him, "Lord, if You had been here, my brother would not have died."

Therefore, when Jesus saw her weeping, and the Jews who came with her weeping, He groaned in the spirit and was troubled. And He said, "Where have you laid him?" They said to Him, "Lord, come and see." Jesus wept. Then the Jews said, "See how He loved him!" And some of them said, "Could not this Man, who opened the eyes of the blind, also have kept this man from dying?" Then Jesus, again groaning in Himself, came to the tomb. It was a cave, and a stone lay against it. Jesus said, "Take away the stone."

Martha, the sister of him who was dead, said to Him, "Lord, by this time there is a stench, for he has been dead four days." Jesus said to her, "Did I not say to you that if you would believe you would see the glory of God?"

Then they took away the stone from the place where the dead man was lying. And Jesus lifted up His eyes and said, "Father, I thank You that You have heard Me. And I know that You always hear Me, but because of the people who are standing by I said this, that they may believe that You sent Me." Now when He had said these things, He cried with a loud voice, "Lazarus, come forth!" And he who had died came out bound hand and foot with grave clothes, and his face was wrapped with a cloth. Jesus said to them, "Loose him, and let him go." (John 11:1-44)

In the Hebrew language, Lazarus is an abbreviation of Eleazar, which means "whom God helps." A principle that we see here is that the person whom God helps must understand there is a purpose behind the help. Purpose is often attached to advancing the kingdom of God in some capacity. The raising of Lazarus plays a key role in the theological and the historical account of Jesus' ministry. It is referred to as the greatest of the series of "signs" Jesus performs. Consider this: Lazarus had been dead and buried for four days.

According to popular Jewish belief, the spirit of a dead person does not desert the body until three days after death. Lazarus was dead. He was not enjoying a deep sleep nor was he in a coma. *He was dead.* Lazarus' resurrection becomes the event that determines the decision of the Jewish authorities to put Jesus to death.

Some of you may ask, how I can compare myself to Lazarus. Let us look at some things he and I have in common. We were dead. Lazarus was dead in his body to his family and friends, but not to God. If God had already declared him dead, this resurrection would have been a contradiction and God does not contradict Himself.

I was dead in my soul and spirit to my family, friends, and the will of God, but God had not declared me dead to Him. If He had done so, I would not have been able to apply the blood and the works of Jesus into my life, without which there is no power to resurrect a life unto God.

To be dead is to be deprived of life; lacking power to move, feel, or respond; incapable of being stirred emotionally or intellectually; barren; no longer producing or functioning; no longer having interest, relevance, or significance. Although I was still breathing, I was deprived of life, moving day to day surviving for the next high. I was unable to tap into the power to move from people and places I needed to move from, to feel anything other than the need to get high. Even when feelings of shame, guilt, condemnation, and fear would come over me, they only led me to the desire to get high.

In this state, I was incapable of being influenced emotionally or intellectually by family, friends, pastors, or counselors. My existence was barren and purposeless. My childhood interests and the things that held significance to me had faded away in the sea of passing memories. Indeed, as Lazarus, I too was dead.

1. Lazarus and I were placed in tombs. Tombs were elaborate burial places for the dead. Niches were carved out to hold the individual bodies of dead family members. When decay reduced the body to bones, the

remains were placed elsewhere in the tomb to make room for new bodies. This refers to generational replacement operating in the tombs. I was right in line for my generational spot in the tomb of substance addiction in my bloodline.

Natural tombs were usually at a distance from the places where the living dwelt. As painful as it was, I understand why people who truly were concerned about me could not allow me to dwell among them. Tombs, not homes, are for the dead. My lifestyle was so far from those "of the norm" that a gap of understanding, relationship, and concern was created. This made understanding relationships, and acts of concern unattainable between many others and myself.

2. Tombs are interesting places. They are comprised of the sicknesses, weaknesses, and lifestyles of sin in our lives. They are places of darkness, isolation, and death. Many of us entered the tombs of our lives seeking shelter or defense. I first entered my tomb attempting to escape the realities of my life. Some of us were placed in tombs because others pronounced us dead. You know those pronouncements from frustrated parents, hateful or ignorant teachers, and bitter associates that proclaimed you were "no good," "just like your no-good father," "a whore like your mother," "too stupid, too poor, too black, too brown, too yellow."

Some of you reading this can realize now that you are in a tomb. Do not be discouraged. Resurrection is available for you. Also keep this thought in mind; ordinary people were buried in shallow graves covered by stones. But people of importance were placed in tombs. If you are in a tomb, that means the enemy wants to make sure your bondage is secure. This means your resurrection cannot come easy for you. You have a powerful purpose to fulfill in the kingdom of God.

3. The third thing Lazarus and I have in common is that Jesus came to our tombs. There is also another account I need to bring into this particular point of commonality. It is the account of when Jesus encountered the two demon-possessed men who lived in the tombs.

These men were not physically dead; therefore, they did not require resurrection, but deliverance. What these two men have in common with Lazarus and me is that Jesus came to them while they were trapped among the tombs. Let's get familiar with the account.

> On the same day, when evening had come, He said to them, "Let us cross over to the other side." Now when they had left the multitude, they took Him along in the boat as He was. And other little boats were also with Him. And a great windstorm arose, and the waves beat into the boat, so that it was already filling. But He was in the stern, asleep on a pillow. And they awoke Him and said to Him, "Teacher, do You not care that we are perishing?"
>
> Then He arose and rebuked the wind, and said to the sea, "Peace, be still!" And the wind ceased and there was a great calm. But He said to them, "Why are you so fearful? How is it that you have no faith?" And they feared exceedingly, and said to one another, "Who can this be, that even the wind and the sea obey Him!"
>
> Then they came to the other side of the sea, to the country of the Gadarenes. And when He had come out of the boat, immediately there met Him out of the tombs a man with an unclean spirit, who had his dwelling among the tombs; and no one could bind him, not even with chains, because he had often been bound with shackles and chains. And the chains had been pulled apart by him, and the shackles broken in pieces; neither could anyone tame him. And always, night and day, he was in the mountains and in the tombs, crying out and cutting himself with stones. (Mark 4:35-5:5)

This account starts on the same day Jesus taught the "parables of the kingdom." He had been feeding the disciples (the church) the Word. When our bodies are fed natural foods, the food goes through a process within our digestive system. The digestive system is composed of a series of connected organs whose purpose is to break down, or digest, the food. The food molecules can then be absorbed into the bloodstream. The simple molecules travel through the bloodstream to all of the body's cells, which use them for growth, repair, and energy.

There is a similar process when we partake of spiritual food, the Word of God. It needs to be digested, broken down and prepared to be put into action. To assist in this process, trials, tests, training, and tribulations are used.

Jesus had fed the disciples, and now comes the process of digestion. The hearing of God's Word is the first step toward faith. It is not enough for us to learn a lesson or be able to repeat a teaching. We must also be able to practice that lesson by faith. Here we see Jesus using the sea to help in the digestion of the Word He had fed them.

In connecting the dots here, we have Jesus feeding the church. What He fed them needed to be broken down and absorbed into their spirits because they would need it to accompany them on the upcoming assignment. Therefore, He allows, or maybe causes, them to enter into a storm at sea to provide the action needed and produce the faith needed to do what Jesus desired to do. It was Jesus' desire to "cross over to the other side."

I believe it is still His desire today for believers to come out from behind the walls of safety and comfort, which our churches provide, and get into the communities they serve to witness and minister to the people where they are, as opposed to just trying to get them to come to church. Transporting urban-centered youth and the homeless to our buildings is not a bad thing. The determining factor is why we are doing it. Could it be that the process or journey involved with crossing over will require us to confront some storms along the way? I am referring to personal storms that can expose our true level of faith, love, commitment, courage, trust, and service.

It was not until Jesus gave the charge to cross over that the disciples found themselves in the middle of a storm and a heart check. It is vital, before stepping into territory filled with demonic forces, generational bloodline curses, and influences that we engage in a heart check. If we don't, we can find ourselves needing to be resurrected and delivered from among the tombs.

Going to the other side was not a light assignment. When Jesus stepped out of the boat, He was confronted and challenged. This man, destined to have an encounter with Jesus, could not be successfully bound morally, religiously, legally or physically. No one could bind him. His family and friends attempted to help him with tough love, self-help programs, institutions, groups, hospitals, and even religion. But none of these things was able to bind him from his self-destruction. All hope of helping him had been abandoned. Out of his agony of physical and spiritual imprisonment, he would cry out and cut himself with stones.

Many nights I walked the streets filled with tears, silently crying from the pain of cutting myself with stones of self-condemnation, self-hatred and self-torment. This man, who dwelt among the tombs, was angry and violent. The anger and violence could have been more of a reaction to the condition he found himself in than a part of his true character. Physical affliction, loneliness, and emotional turmoil filled his life. He lived among the graves of dead people and other outcasts of society. The surrounding mountains were hiding places for criminals and dwelling places for the poor and insane, just as many of the urban areas within our society are.

It was a dead environment and a burial site of thousands of dreams, visions, ideals, and hopes. It contained stockpiles of unused and untapped gifts and abilities. You cannot dwell among the dead and not start dying mentally, spiritually, and emotionally yourself. It is Satan's desire to have us dwelling in dead environments. This gives more strength to demonic bondages because it isolates the inhabitants from the power of the resurrection and the life. We know this power to be in the person of Jesus of Nazareth. It represents the holistic ministry the church is charged to submit to the world. Coming out of tombs requires both resurrection and life.

Without the Christ, there would have been no resurrection. The term resurrection refers to "the act of rising from the dead or returning to life; the state of one raised from the dead." Resurrection is to be distinguished from resuscitation or reanimation of the physical body. It denotes a complete transformation of the human being in his or her psychosomatic totality, or in other words a transformation that involves both the mind and body.

On the third day, Jesus Christ was raised from the dead. The resurrection declares Jesus Christ to be the Son of God. The resurrection of those dead in trespasses and sin declares the continual work of the Son of God in our lives today. To be chosen to bear witness that Jesus, the Christ, is alive is a wonderful blessing.

Life, as translated from the Greek word *zoë* is "the state of one who is possessed of a life both essential and ethical, which belongs to and is devoted to God. It is possible to be resurrected, but not have life (zoe). Life is God's basic blessing (see Deut. 30:19). Sometimes life means not only survival but also well-being (see Prov. 3:13-18). In Deuteronomy and wisdom literature, life is associated with keeping the commandments of God. The New Testament expanded on the Old Testament idea of life. The word *life* began to refer to more than physical existence. It took on a strong spiritual meaning, often referring to the spiritual life that results from our relationship with God.

Too many believers have settled for resurrection. We settle with being freed from various habits, bondages, and weaknesses. Being free from bondage to drugs, alcoholic, shopping, gambling, sex, and pornography is a wonderful blessing. Without the life (that which reveals purpose and brings connection, relationship, and devotion to God), we are zombies, walking around dead to our past actions but still alive to the character it developed within us.

Many times when I stopped using drugs (once for as long as two-and-a-half years), within me the drug-addicted character was still operating. I was still being dishonest, untrustworthy, fearful, untrusting, manipulative, and isolated. In many ways, I replaced crack cocaine with religion. It was my new hiding place from the issues in my life. The good thing about it was its acceptability. Even "religious freak" had a better ring to it than "crack head." Today I thank and praise God for providing and allowing me to walk in the resurrection and the life.

Ride with me now through the streets, tunnels, alleys, systems, and institutions that brought me to my current position in life and relationship with God. To Him and Him alone is the glory. Let's ride . . .

Chapter 2

The Altering of My Mind

I WAS BORN in Newark, New Jersey, in the Central Ward. I attended Central Avenue School, which was located about a mile from where we lived on First Street. Walking to school, my friends and I would pass the Cadillac dealership, a rubber factory, and an ice cream production plant (I remember when the warehouse moved out after the riots we would go inside and find left-behind ice cream in the freezers. That was one of our consolation gifts from a burned-down community). I also passed a supermarket, the National Guard Armory, and two "shooting galleries," depending on which way we walked. For those who may not know, "shooting galleries" were places where users would go to shoot heroin and/or cocaine into their bodies. They were equivalent to the "crack houses" of today.

As a ten-year-old child, I was always thinking of ways to get money, other than stealing it from my parents. I used the businesses I walked by every day to develop my own businesses. I established four of them: I shined shoes at the local Cadillac dealership, carried groceries at Good Deals supermarket, sold candy in school that I bought from the wholesale candy shop around the corner from where we lived, and I helped heroin addicts find that second vein to inject heroin when they could not. They would pay fifty cents to a dollar for the service. This is how I was introduced to heroin. Between the ages of ten and twelve I had already experimented or consistently used cigarettes, wine, beer, liquors, as well as sniffing glue and spot remover and taking pills and heroin.

My first mind-altering experience came through a cheap wine called "Orange-So-Good." We would pay the local alcoholics to go into the liquor store and buy it for us. Soon I progressed to "Boone's Farm Apple Wine," "Thunderbird," and stealing the small airplane bottles of whisky from my father's supply at home. I remember one time I took a couple of the small bottles to school. We would drink them in the coat room. This particular day, I placed the empty bottle in my back pocket. I was going to throw it away outside of the classroom.

My friends were choosing teams for touch football, so I ran to get in the crowd to be chosen. In the course of playing, I was knocked down to the ground and fell on my butt. You know what happened, right? The bottle broke and I had to get stitches. Of course the school nurse asked me what happened. My ten-year-old ingenious mind developed a story that would make me a hero. Since I was a "patrol boy" (for those who may not know, a patrol boy or girl helped monitor the halls, playground, and crossing corners near the school), I told the nurse that I was patrolling the playground and found a broken piece of glass and put it in my pocket so none of the other kids would get hurt. Looking back now, I am sure the nurse was laughing and thinking, *I can't wait to call his mom with this one.* When my mother arrived at the school, her concern quickly shifted to anger and embarrassment. In spite of what had happened, she still covered me from the wrath of my father by not telling him what really happened. She was probably worried that between the glass tearing up one side and my father tear up the other, I would have no butt at all.

My wine and alcohol experience continued, as the neighborhood alcoholics (we called them winos) would buy the wine for us as long as we had enough money to buy some for them too. Looking back, it really saddens me because now I can understand the pain and regret many of them were dealing with. Especially those we called "watchers." They would position themselves somewhere on the block and watch what was going on in the neighborhood when they were not passed out from drinking.

One, who we called Porter, always impressed me. He was like the neighborhood father, counselor, and teacher. He was the best storyteller I had ever heard, and he loved to talk about history. He and a few others were our ghetto wise men, who would sit at the gate and discuss all kinds of topics. Often before Porter would go to the liquor store for us, we would have to listen to him pour out whatever concern was on his mind. I would never tell anyone but I enjoyed him talking to me. He always left me with something to think about or something I did not know before. Also, I believe I just liked the ideal that at least one man on the block cared about me. I think he and a few others were trying to make right with us what went wrong with their own children. Amazing that at this moment, Porter is still teaching me lessons. His life on the block and my reaction to it demonstrate the natural power and need for a man to a boy; a father to a son relationship.

This relationship is so powerful and needed that it will find a way to manifest itself even in the midst of conscious withdrawal from life. To every father reading this book, think about this: If a male child who is so starved for the attention of a man can obtain a sense of care and covering from a drunk who yells at him to "stop running in the street before you get hit by a car" or questions him on why he is not in school, how much more would that affect him coming from you.

A time came when we did not need adults to buy wine or malt liquor for us anymore. One of my friends lived in an apartment building where his parents were the superintendents of the building. They allowed us to have an area in the basement for our "clubhouse." That was prime real estate for twelve- and thirteen-year-olds in the hood. We fixed it up with old furniture and other knickknacks we found. Some items were given to us by other adults in the neighborhood who were happy to help us settle anywhere other than their porch, car, or backyard.

The best feature of our clubhouse was one of its walls. This wall separated the basement of the apartment building from the basement of the bar that was below the apartments. It did not take us long to figure out the jackpot we had just fallen into. Yes, we punched out a hole in the wall and helped ourselves to the supplies of liquor stored in the basement. Not only did we bypass the middle man, we became the man. We started selling liquor to the kids and adults. We had it all, including what was then the ghetto champagne, "cold duck."

As a child, I could fit into different groups in the area. It seemed that each group was doing something different. I was drinking with one group and sniffing glue and spot remover with another group. It was with this group that I added stealing from retail stores. We would go into Good Deal Supermarket and steal spot remover. We would pour the remover onto a rag or handkerchief, place it over our nose and mouth, and inhale.

One night while out getting high using remover, I had placed my rag into the pocket of my brand-new leather coat my mother had just bought me. I lit a cigarette and I was so high that when I needed to tie my shoe, I put the cigarette in my pocket. The rag caught on fire. I remembered how everything was in slow motion, even sounds. Therefore, when my friends tried to tell me my coat was on fire, by the time it registered and I reacted to their screaming, the heat had destroyed the whole side of my new leather jacket. By the grace of God, I was not injured. The more I look back over my life, I find evidence of the truth of the statement that "God watches over babes and fools." I was no baby at this time.

My drug using adventure reached a very dark point when I started shooting heroin. Heroin provided the longest means of escape for me. Unlike the pills I used to take, which often made me feel sick, heroin provided a peaceful drift into nothingness. This drift took me deeper and deeper as I moved from inhaling, to skin-popping (injecting the drug just underneath the skin for quicker flow into the bloodstream), to mainlining (injecting directly into the bloodstream via a vein). This method is also known as intravenous injection. It provides the greatest intensity and most rapid onset of euphoria (seven to eight seconds), while sniffing or smoking it took about ten to fifteen minutes for the effects to be felt.

Smoking heroin was not very popular in my community during the period of my addiction to it. I was able to maintain my supply of heroin by stealing money from my home, running errands for neighbors and drug dealers, and hustling at Good Deal Supermarket.

The more of the drug I used, the greater my dependency on the drug grew. This dependence was completely physical. If drug use is reduced abruptly, the body, which has adapted to the presence of the drug, withdrawal symptoms occur. The withdrawal symptoms empowered the drive to obtain more of the drug "by any means necessary." My symptoms included restlessness, muscle and bone pain, insomnia, diarrhea, vomiting, cold flashes with goose bumps, and involuntary leg movements.

My addiction to heroin lasted for about eight or nine months before my cold turkey withdrawal of the drug out of my body. I did not have the luxury of enduring this process in a professional setting or hospital. It was four days and three nights of hell locked in a bedroom. The physical pain was like nothing I had felt before. All I could do was ball up as tight as possible and cry myself to sleep. However, the sleep did not last long. I would wake up only to consciously begin the painful process again. Even today, some forty years later, I still cannot look at any type of needle entering my skin.

Although my use of heroin stopped, I quickly found a few other chemical friends. Pills were much easier to take and less costly. In the street, we referred to them as gorilla pills because of the violent and bold state in which they placed a person. The biggest coward on the block could take a couple of "red devils" and turn into the Terminator, all the X-Men, Tupac, Superfly, and Captain America (someone my senior readers can relate to).

The effects of taking the various pills that were available worked well for me. They gave me the courage I needed to overcome my shyness with females and ignore my shuddering problem. I still do not understand how the various pills I used—codeine, amphetamines, and barbiturates—which were known to cause relaxation and sleepiness, had an opposite effect on me. The sad part was I was becoming addicted to another chemical that provided me an instant, temporary solution that I could have resolved myself if I had only been taught how to. I realize now that most, if not all, of my drug use, were results of my inability to cope with and resolve emotional issues. Without drugs, I had two ways of dealing with emotional issues—ignore them or get violent and both are bad choices.

Another drug I experimented with during this period of my life was methadone. This was the drug of choice if one was trying to kick heroin addiction. Methadone provided the same type of high as heroin and would stop the withdrawal pains. It was not as addicting and lasted much longer. For me, methadone had an unsettling history that helped me to stop using it quickly. It was developed in response to an order by Hitler to develop an alternative to morphine, which was in short supply at the end of World War II. The trade name Dolophine is recorded to have been derived from Hitler's first name Adolph. Furthermore, I did not like the fact that it came as a liquid.

I think what I enjoyed most was the excitement connected with buying the drug. A friend's sister was a heavy heroin user who would use "meth" in between. I learned about the drug from her. Sometimes we would ride with her to Harlem, New York, to get it. I have always been in love with New York. I cannot recall the how and why of it, but from my childhood to this very day I love New York. I always felt like a part of me had been there before and belongs there.

Sometimes we would drive; other times we would take the Path to New York, then the subway uptown. The Path was a train that ran from Penn Station, Newark, to the World Trade Center in New York. I remember how excited I would get rising up out of the subway tunnel to the streets. Amsterdam Avenue and 116th Street was our stop. On the way back, my friend's sister often stopped at a certain bar while we waited outside. My friend was big, but only fifteen years old. I was only thirteen. His sister would take us because she did not like to go by herself. We stood outside, looking as "hard" as we could, hoping nobody would try us. After a few trips, I became more comfortable going there. I felt at home. Little did I know a few years later I would be living a few blocks from that same corner.

From the ages of fourteen to about twenty, my drug of choice was marijuana. I smoked it every day. It became my new source of enablement. When I needed to be social, intelligent, creative, funny, scholarly, or whatever, a little reefer did the job for me. During that period of my life, I had become deeply involved in the Nation of Islam. There was no way I could be on some corner nodding out without some serious physical repercussions. Image was a big thing in the Nation. Although many of the members were still struggling with the social use of drugs, many would go to places away from public view to use them.

I was twenty when I started my use of drugs that pumped you up not down. These drugs caused the seeing of images, the hearing of sounds, and the feelings of sensations that were not real. What I enjoyed most about them was how they affected my hearing of music. My new escape from day-to-day living was dance clubs, reefer, THC and Mescaline when I started my recreational use of cocaine. I moved quickly from the occasional user to a dealer, to what we called a kitchen chemist, to being my best customer, to being completely consumed in freebasing, what later became popular as smoking crack. Of my entire drug using history, this addiction was the longest, hardest, and most destructive I have ever faced. I was dead on so many different levels that only through the grace of God, the work of Jesus Christ, and the power of the Holy Spirit could I be revived back to any sense of life as we know it.

Chapter 3

Nation Time

IN THE NEIGHBORHOOD I grew up in, there were a candy store, a liquor store, and a church on every block. There was a church on the corner of Central Avenue and First Street that used to be jumping on Friday night. I think that was the only time we paid it any attention. In the summer, they would have the front doors open. You could hear the music down the block. We would be getting high in the alley down the street, dancing to the music that flowed outside. I used to think that the church was not for us. I did not know anybody on our street who attended there.

As a Christian now looking back, I find it sad that of the three storefront churches that were there, none of them followed their music out of the doors and into the alleys, hallways, and abandoned buildings to share their "good news" and to reach out to the individuals who seemed to be stuck there. Was the music so loud that it drowned out the muffled cries for help and attention?

While they were in their building having their meeting, the Nation of Islam took to the streets, helping their children. It was men from the Nation who pulled me out of the heroin den and helped get me off the drug.

At the age of twelve, the Nation of Islam affected my life greatly. The Nation was the first place I consistently observed African-American men in a positive light. They walked, dressed, and talked in a manner that commanded respect, and I wanted to copy that. In addition, it appeared that they were the only ones who were willing to come into the dark areas of the community and bring people out. They cleaned me up, educated me, acknowledged and addressed my pain and anger, and gave me a sense of purpose. I will always be grateful for the role the Nation of Islam played in changing my life and getting me off heroin. However, I realize that this was only window dressing and cover-up. My anger and inability to handle certain emotional issues were still influencing my life. That is why I continued to smoke reefer and occasionally use other drugs. This was always done in isolation.

Soon after my heroin cleanup, my sister Dorothy was the first in the family to join the Nation of Islam. I soon followed behind her. In order to become a member, you had to copy a pre-written out letter to the Honorable Elijah Muhammad. The letter had to be copied exactly as it was pre-written. I had to write my letter about four or five times before it was finally accepted.

Looking at it now, in the application process we were being groomed to simply copy what we were being taught and trained. After receiving my acceptance letter, I took it to the Temple I would be joining. Temple #25 on South Orange Avenue, Newark, New Jersey. My sister served as the Secretary of the Temple. The day I received my "X" was the first time I sensed my sister being proud of me. I was now to be referred to as Brother Kevin 12X. The number twelve meant that I was the twelfth Kevin to become a member of Temple 25.

I find it interesting that in Judeo-Christian teachings, the number twelve represents a foundation. The discipline, desire, and need to study and pray would be the foundation I would be able to build my faith in Jesus Christ and His teachings upon.

I think because of my sister's position, I got deeply involved in the Nation very quickly. I loved the ideal of studying and learning things none in my age group had knowledge of. The best times of my day would be when I had a group of people around doing what we called "kicking the science." This is when we would share our knowledge, insights, and understanding. I really enjoyed it when I would win a debate over an adult. It was twice as rewarding when on "fishing" assignments, I was able to win over an adult. Churches refer to it as "witnessing"; others ring your doorbell early in the morning. The Nation referred to it as fishing for new members. We did a combination of things: home visits, standing on corners, etc.

One of my favorites was when I was assigned to a team focused on Sunday morning church worshippers. I even had a favorite church. I cannot recall the name. It was located on Central Avenue and 8ᵗʰ Street. The pastor was Rev. Skinner. I had developed to the point where I was very successful in recruiting from this particular group. I think because I was so young, the adults were less careful in engaging with me, and I studied my materials daily. One of the first questions I would ask the individual was to give me their opinion of what the preacher had talked about. Then I would ask how could that be applied to their social conditions. Then I would share the teachings of Elijah Muhammad regarding these conditions.

Once that door was open, I could control the conversation. Another successful approach was to question them on their loyalty to Jesus and His teachings. Once I had them defending their commitment to Jesus, almost to the point of being willing to prove it, I would ask them to explain John 14:15-16: "If you love me, you will keep my commandments. And I will ask the Father, and he will give you another Advocate, to be with you forever." The King James Version uses the word *Comforter* for Advocate. I would ask them to define what a comforter is. Then I would ask who is this Comforter Jesus was teaching about? Most did not have a clue on how to respond to my questions. I would then go on to explain that the Comforter Jesus taught about was Elijah Muhammad. And if they really believed in Jesus' teaching they would be followers of Muhammad. I must admit that a great deal of my confidence was in the fact that most Christians do not read and study the Bible for themselves. Therefore, they would be unequipped for effective debate.

As a junior Fruit of Islam (FOI), my responsibilities grew quickly, but not as fast as my brother's did. Upon his return from Vietnam with some help from my mom, sister, and I, my brother also joined the Nation. My brother's training in the Army Special Forces quickly made room for him in the FOI. He assisted in combat training of the FOI, among other things. I got additional training from him, which allowed me to surpass others in junior FOI training classes.

I remember when I first got my FOI uniform. I walked around the house with it on all day. Checking myself out in the mirror making sure I looked worthy enough to have it on. My fez was a little big so my sister altered it for me. For my sister to offer to do anything for me was amazing. We were always fighting before my joining the Nation. I was promoted to the position of Junior Squad Leader. I was also allowed to attend the adult FOI training classes. This was a big honor. I made sure I never missed a class and was always on time.

Soon I was holding posts and positions only adults or older teenagers held. I started with outside observations during services. I would be stationed on a corner, in a car, or on the roof, looking for suspicious activity. Then I moved to inside observation, sitting among the attendees. My next to favorite post was the security search for weapons, cameras, and recording devices. This was a huge responsibility for one of my age and I approached it that way. I practiced the search skills on friends and went over them with my brother. The goal was to be complete from head to toe and fast.

As my training in combat and self-defense improved, I was selected to hold the front security post. This was the most important position of security inside the Temple. It required the most discipline and skill. We had to sit absolutely still with only eye movement scanning the audience. Left hand had to be on your left thigh covered by the right hand. Because I was always the student, it was difficult for me at first to tune out what the minister was teaching.

Fruit of Islam was a subsystem within the Nation of Islam focused on development and order. Classes were held starting at 7:00 a.m. on Saturday mornings to help develop men in every area of life. Self-defense (karate, judo, kick-boxing), finances, business, family values, health, historical and political awareness, culture, self-respect, honor, and pride were some of the topics covered. The training also stressed high work ethics, high morals, and a disciplined mind, body, and spirit. As men it was drilled into us that honor meant more than life. The two things we were to honor most were Elijah Muhammad and our women. We were taught that how we treat our women and the women's behavior were the hallmarks of being viewed as a cultured, dignified, person in the eyes of other nations. Members of the FOI handled charges of domestic abuse and any type of disrespect of our women. If required, additional help, education, and counsel were provided to the family. Sometimes these interventions were not pretty. But they got the message across.

The women also had mandatory classes they had to attend on Saturday afternoons after the FOI classes. Their classes were known as MGT-GCC (Muslim Girls Training & General Civilization Class). The women studied cooking, sewing, religion, hygiene, creating a proper home environment, raising children, duties as a wife, and social behavior. One of the things that gave me a great sense of pride during this period in my life was to see the respect Muslim women were receiving in the community. Even the drug addicts and drunks would stop in their tracks in respect to these women. If my mom or sisters were out after dark, I never worried about their well-being. If a Muslim man saw a Muslim woman in the street after dark, she was to be escorted to her destination.

The Nation developed its own school for the children, the University of Islam. Sister Claire Muhammad, wife of Elijah Muhammad, developed the school. It started as an elementary and secondary school that grew into a high school. The curriculum focused on mathematics, science, astronomy, religion, and African-American history. I envied those who could attend the university. I wanted to attend but my father could not afford to send me. Elijah Muhammad, who was believed to be "the last Messenger of God," led the Nation of Islam. He taught a mixture of Middle Eastern Islamic teachings, black nationalism, and psychology. I believe if he had come to African-American men and women with pure Islamic teaching, he would not have attracted the number of followers he did. Islam was introduced as the original religion of the black man.

One of the books we were required to read was *The Miseducation of the Negro* by Dr. Carter G. Woodson. In this book, Dr. Woodson stated, "The program for the uplift of the Negro in this country must be based upon a scientific study of the Negro from within to develop in him the power to do for himself what his oppressors will never do to elevate him to the level of others" (pg.144). This is what the theology of the Nation of Islam attempted to address.

Elijah Muhammad was born Elijah Poole. Born in Sandersville, Georgia, in 1897, Poole's formal education ended with elementary school. At age ten, he witnessed the lynching of a black man. At fourteen, he joined the Baptist church. In 1923, Poole migrated to Detroit with his wife and two children, where he became a factory worker. An individual known as W. D. Fard introduced him to this teaching. He taught Elijah that Yakub, a black scientist, created the white race and that Allah had allowed this devilish race to hold power for 6,000 years. Their time was up in 1914, and the twentieth century was to be the time for black people to assert themselves.

This myth supported a program of economic self-sufficiency, the development of black-owned businesses, and a demand for the creation of a separate black nation to be carved out of the states of Georgia, Alabama, and Mississippi. Elijah also encouraged his followers to drop their "slave" names in favor of Muslim names or, in most cases, an X, signifying that they had lost their identities in slavery and did not know their true names. We were taught that we were the lost tribe of Shabazz in the wilderness of North America.

The organization came at odds with mainstream Islam, civil rights advocates, as well as the United States government. Although the organization is not accepted by mainstream Islam, it thrives with blacks who were at the bottom of society. The organization did and continues to reform black drug addicts, pimps, hustlers, hookers, criminals, and others that the black church, social services, mainstream Islam, and others could not reach. The organization was also able to build a separate black economy that included mosques, barbershops, grocery stores, schools, bakeries, dry cleaners, farms, banks, and a successful whiting fish operation in the majority of the major cities of America.

Between 1971 and 1974, a lot of bloodshed took place in which the members of the Nation of Islam were involved. In Newark, much of this violence was the result of fighting between the Nation of Islam and two of its spinoff groups, New World Nation of Islam (NWNOI) and the Five Percenters. Some former members of the Newark Temple started the NWNOI in early 1960. The leader of this group was arrested for bank robbery around 1965. He continued to run the group from Trenton State Prison where he was sentenced to serve his time. He recruited many of the inmates there and the group's influence spread through the New Jersey prison system and the ghetto areas, just as the Nation of Islam had.

The Five Percenters were the brainchildren of an expelled Nation of Islam member from Temple #7 in Harlem. He was known to associate with various street gangs. Out of this association, he started his own group known as the Five Percenters. They believed that 85 percent of African-Americans were blind and ignorant to the truth. Ten percent was completely sold out and cared nothing about our community, including preachers and politicians. This left only 5 percent having the true knowledge, wisdom, and understanding of God. The claim was that they were that 5 percent. This group spread throughout the New York prison system and the streets of metropolitan New York/New Jersey.

In October 1971, Raymond Sharrief, captain of Newark's Temple #25, was the target of a failed assassination attempt. The captain was responsible for the training, security, organization, and function of the FOI. It was believed that the attempt was carried out by the NWNOI in a plan to get control of Temple #25. After the attempt on his life, Mr. Sharrief moved his family to Baltimore.

My brother stepped in to assist in these areas. My brother was born Jesse Reddick, Jr. Upon his assignment in the Nation, he took on the name Mustafa Muhammad. In fact, many of us discarded our X and took on names. I must admit I felt a sense of belonging to a people, culture, and history beyond the American experience when I changed my name. I kept my first name because my mother gave it to me. I gave myself the middle name of Shaheed (one who upholds the first pillar of faith) and took the same last name as my brother, Muhammad. Because I was still a minor, I could not change my name legally. By the time I reached the age to do so, my thinking and concerns were starting to shift.

A year later, I was given what we within the FOI considered an honor post, security detail at the home of our chief minister, James Shabazz. It was an evening detail outside of his home. I was positioned in a car with another brother. We would alternate walking the block and around the house. I think that night was the first time I had coffee. I was wired.

Every little sound and movement was suspect. Not just because of the coffee, but also due to the tension that was in the city.

About two weeks after my detail, Minister Shabazz was assassinated by former members of the Nation of Islam, who then belonged to the New World of Islam's group out of East Orange, New Jersey. He was shot in the face outside of his home in the morning on his way to the Temple. I recall walking up Central Avenue and Market Street when some brother drove up to me and told me about the murder. I wanted to just drop to my knees and cry, but I knew I could not. That was quickly replaced with rage.

I was told to get in the car because it was not safe for me to be walking the streets alone, and we went directly to the Temple. Although I had been mentally prepared for "warfare," this just did not feel right. I was expecting my enemy to be the white man, not my brothers of the same color. At the time, I was fourteen years old. My mother sat up at night worrying when I was not home. A dark change was taking place in an already dark community. This could not continue.

Minister Shabazz's assassination led to the subsequent murders and decapitations of four members of the NWOI. Their heads were discovered in a park on the south side of the city and their bodies in Westside Park, not far from the minister's home.

For the first few weeks after all of the violence, I isolated myself. I was trying to wrap my head around all that had just happened. But my family and friends did not allow me to stay isolated long. Soon I was back to business as normal.

My interest in attending high school was football. My brother was a star football player at Central High School. My plan was to follow my brother's footsteps and play high school football. Due to what I believed at the time to be fate, my mother and I moved to 10th Street after I graduated from Alexander Street Elementary School in the Vailsburg section of Newark. This was my third elementary school due to my being expelled from the other two.

My wife often teases me, saying I am the only person she knows who was kicked out of two elementary schools. I was expelled from Central Avenue for throwing a piece of wood from my shop class at my teacher. From there, I attended Sussex Avenue School for about a year before I was expelled for bringing alcohol into the school. My mother and I also had moved outside of the school district, which gave them additional ground to expel me. My events led me to Alexander Street School. I regret that my eighth grade graduation was with a complete group of strangers, but it was my own doing.

Moving to 10th Street provided the address I needed to attend Barringer High School. Barringer had the best football program and a winning record in the city at that time. It was the Central High of my brother's day. What better school for me to play football in, following after my brother.

My friend Robert and I were in the tryouts for the Junior Varsity squad. I was trying for the position of strong safety and fullback. Robert was going after defensive and tight end positions. On the day the lines were being selected, Robert was picked for both positions on both the junior varsity and varsity teams. He would be starting in the junior line-up and second string on the varsity team. I really got excited about this because I believed I was a better quality player that he was. He was bigger, but I was faster and stronger. I knew I would be making one, if not both teams.

In my excitement, I shared this news with a fellow squad leader in the Nation. Soon I was summoned and informed that as a Muslim I could not be involved in "sport and play" in the white man's school system. I felt I had no choice but to let go of my dream of playing football.

With my major interest in school dead to me, and my opinion of and value placed on the educational system at an all-time low, I slowly dropped out of school. I say slowly because I stopped going to classes a class at a time. I got to a point where I went to school and hung out in the cafeteria. It was there that a few other Nation followers and I would hold our own class at the corner table. I loved to debate. I would sit up at night studying for the debates of the following day. We operated as unofficial debate teams. We had not had structured training of debating as seen in the movie "The Great Debaters," but that was how we operated. There would be little or no yielding, cursing, or disrespectful language.

Opinions that were shared by a member of the Nation had to be followed by some form of scholarship, a supporting statement by another wiser than we were on the subject. I believe that was one of the things that gave my opinions such a welcoming by others and credibility. The only reason I would read the Bible then was to find and memorize a passage of Scripture that would support the opinion I was sharing. Some days that was what I did all day, going from one location to the next, debating and discussing. (Side note – I now understand that this part of my development as a youth was the main reason I struggled so hard with preachers who did the loud breathing, yelling, and spitting. I could not intelligently follow what was being shared due to all the emotional overtones that distracted my attention. That is still a struggle for me today.)

We would discuss any subject that came up, challenge what was being taught in some of the classes, and debate the "truth" taught by Elijah Muhammad and the "lie" taught by the white man. A very interesting thing about the cafeteria situation was that the school administration allowed it. The security officers actually welcomed us on the campus. The other students followed an established atmosphere set by us of respect and order. The group would check any activity that belittled self-respect, respect toward females, and those in authority immediately.

We were greatly appreciated by the students in the months before the end of school. Like other schools, Barringer had its share of racial tension. The school was located in Branch Brook Park, one of the largest parks in the city. It was also right on the borderline of two different neighborhoods. There were the Italians and the Blacks and Puerto Ricans. The Italians would wait to catch individuals walking home from school and jump them. Between members of the Nation and two gangs from the 7th Avenue projects, we would escort students through the park and down Park Avenue to a safe area. Although we faced several altercations and dangerous situations at the end of the day, I would be overwhelmed with a sense of pride and self-worth. I was someone my community appreciated.

I completely stopped going to classes in the middle of my sophomore year of high school. A friend of the family opened a Muslim sandwich shop known as "Steak-N-Take." Our families grew up together and we referred to each other as cousins. In all the years our families knew each other, I had no idea that they were related to Elijah Muhammad. One of my brother's best friends was actually the nephew of Muhammad. He gave me a job at the shop located on Orange Street in Newark. Soon I worked my way up to assistant manager. The money I made helped establish my independence. At the age of fifteen, I was helping my mother pay bills, buying all my own clothes, food, etc.

At this point, the white man's school for me was definitely outdated and unnecessary. This job also gave me the opportunity to travel to Chicago during our "Savior's Day" celebration. Savior's Day was an annual event in the Nation of Islam where members traveled to Temple #2 in Chicago to pay tribute and honor to Elijah Muhammad. Many cities would rent a large location where several temples could come together and view the service via closed-circuit television for those unable to make the trip. Newark Temple #25 hosted the event for our area at Newark Symphony Hall. All the big events in Newark were held there.

I remember during one Savior's Day I was holding a security post on the roof and I looked over and saw a sea of white (the color of the women's MGT uniform) and blue (the color of the men's FOI uniform) in almost every direction. It was as if we had taken control of the city. I felt as if I truly was different from all the images that were in the media and what I had seen the most of growing up. The stereotype projected onto blacks, even in the early seventies, did not and could not apply to me. The Nation of Islam provided that magic to the black community.

My job at the Steak-N-Take was working out great for me. I was able to add to my income by making my own fruit salad and selling it there. The customers liked the idea that I would change some of the fruits every time I made the salad. My other secret was that I would add some "Shabazz Fruit Cola" to the juice to give the salad a unique flavor.

We were known for our steak and fish sandwiches. The steak sandwiches were made like Philly steaks, except ours were served on a whole wheat roll with "secret" sauce, which was made of ketchup, mustard, and pickle juice. I was especially proud of the fish we sold because they came from the Nation of Islam's fishing company operated in partnership with the government of Peru. We called the fish Whiting H&G. Never knew what the H&G stood for, maybe healthy and good.

The fish were the biggest whitings I had seen. When you butterflied them, they covered a plate. They were so popular in the community that the R & B/Jazz group Kool and the Gang wrote a song entitled "Whiting H&G."

It was through this fish that I met Val. She lived up the street from the store with her younger sister and her mother. Their mother was bound by alcoholism and spent most of her time in the bar below where they lived. Therefore, Val was the one taking care of her little sister and many times her mother. Often Val would come to the restaurant to get something to eat. At the time, Val was a tenth-grade student at Barringer High. I was impressed that she was able to handle the responsibilities in her home, maintain good grades, and be on the cheerleading team. Sometimes when she or her sister came in for a sandwich, they counted out coins and at times were short. I would always look out for them when they were short, give them extra, etc.

Sometimes Val would sit in the restaurant so we could talk. Yes, Val was fine. Her beautiful, dark-skinned face, bright eyes, and fiery spirit were a major attraction for me. My conversations with her included the teachings of Elijah Muhammad. I introduced her to some Muslim women who visited the restaurant. Together we soon had Val and her sister visiting during the services at the Temple and finally becoming a member. Val was now officially my girlfriend. In fact, she was my first girlfriend in the Nation of Islam.

After several months, Val's commitment began to waver. She started challenging and questioning some of the teachings and contradictions that I too would come to face years later. For example, she could not understand how I could be so firm about the need for her to quit cheerleading because of the revealing uniforms, but it was okay for us to have sex.

I think another underlying reason I was so against her cheerleading was resentment. She was a part of the football team, something that I so desired to be a part of myself but could not. Our relationship ended after about a year and a half. The gift Val left me with that I appreciated the most was the courage to question and be open-minded. Little did I know that her gift would lead me to studying the teachings and life of Malcolm X and back into my high school classroom.

The teachings of Malcolm X

My first true exposure to Malcolm X came from a firsthand source. During a Nation event in New York, the FOI from Temple #25 in Newark collaborated with Temple #7 in Harlem to provide security and support. During that event, I met Brother Derrick 27X. Derrick was about three years older than I and in lived in Harlem. That was enough motivation for me to make him my best friend in the Nation.

I would always jump on the train and go to his house and hang out in his neighborhood. That was just so exciting to me.

After meeting Derrick's mother and sharing with her several times about my family and myself, she asked me I knew about Malcolm X? I started repeating what I was informed about him in FOI classes and discussions I listened to, most of which was negative in nature and tone. Therefore, so was my opinion of him.

I knew I had said something she was not pleased with by the anger exploding on her face. At that moment, she started educating me on Malcolm. She gave me a book to read entitled *The Speeches of Malcolm X*. However, what really set off my curiosity about Malcolm was when Derrick's mother introduced me to her sister. She had actually sat under Malcolm's teaching when he was a minister in the Nation and followed him after his split. As Malcolm began to be revealed to me through the firsthand stories, as well as books and tapes, I quickly grew to admire and appreciate his life. My honor and love for Malcolm grew out of his strength, wisdom, and courage to take a stand, not just for lack Muslims, but also for black Americans.

The unbound, fiery words of Malcolm X were not new to blacks in the inner cities. However, when mainstream white America received their first serving of them, the political climate of the civil right movement began to shift. This began in 1959 when Malcolm appeared on the Mike Wallace Show entitled "The Hate That Hate Produced." White America, as were some blacks, was completely shocked and frightened by Malcolm's words. Those who thought Martin Luther King and other leaders within the civil rights movement were dangerous now thought they were lambs compared to the call and accusations of Malcolm. He was radical and intelligent.

Malcolm's labeling of being "anti-white, anti-American, and anti-Christian" placed him in the line of fire of both blacks and whites to discredit his charges. Malcolm loved debating with individuals. I believe the training I received in the art of debating in the Nation of Islam was birthed out of Malcolm's love of it and success with it. In the Amsterdam News, (a black-owned newspaper), Malcolm was called the "giant killer" because of his ability to win debates with powerful leaders in various arenas.

Malcolm was introduced to the Nation of Islam when he was in prison. The Nation of Islam was targeted to the spiritual, social, economic, and political needs of the black underclass, mainly men and women in prisons and urban ghettos. The teachings of Elijah Muhammad addressed one of Malcolm's biggest problems with American Christianity. The religious heroes of the Qur'an and in the teaching of the Nation were individuals of color. Even for me this played a large role in reshaping the image of my people and myself. I often wondered how God, Jesus, angels, and all of the major figures in the Bible were white when the location of many of the recorded events was located on the African continent.

In addition, everything evil, wicked, and negative was associated with black. Malcolm believed this had a negative impact on blacks. During a speech in Camden, New Jersey, Malcolm put forth this challenge to the audience: "Find a black man who has raped a woman . . . who is a drunk, or a black man in the gutter, and you will find a black man who is a Christian."[1]

Malcolm's distaste for Christianity was not a result of his studies of the faith itself. He, as well as other Muslims, believed its doctrine and moral instruction were the closest to those of Islam. He often addressed the practices and actions (or lack thereof) of the people who called themselves Christians.

Malcolm often encouraged his listeners to "go beyond a man's words and examine his deeds." There was also the issue of the white church failure to address racism as a serious religious and social problem. It is often stated that the most segregated hours in America are Sunday mornings. Sadly, it was true then and is still true today. It is a grave mistake to deny the truth of a matter because of how and who may be delivering that truth. Many Christian institutions of learning were brave enough to overcome the fear of seeing an ugly truth in a mirror. They invited Malcolm in to share his points of view. Boston University School of Theology was one of the first. Interesting that the city of Boston was the place where Malcolm was arrested and sentenced to prison. It is believed that a graduate student named C. Eric Lincoln, who became associated with Malcolm during research on his Ph.D. dissertation on black Muslims, was very influential in getting Malcolm an invitation to the university.

Malcolm was also equally disturbed by the images associated with Western Christianity. "Our slave masters gave us a blond, blue-eyed, pale-skinned 'god' for us to worship and admire." He further stated, "The religion of other people makes them proud of who they are, but Christianity was designed to make us look down on black and look up to white. It made blacks feel inferior because we were taught that 'God cursed us black.'"[2]

The shift in Malcolm's thinking and messages began to take shape in December 1963. During a speech Malcolm was presenting on behalf of Elijah Muhammad, he spoke of the topic of "God's judgment of white America." After the speech, he entertained questions from reporters. It was then that he commented on the assassination of President John F. Kennedy as the "chickens coming home to roost," referring to the violence of America. The statement was in reference to the violence blacks, Native Indians and other people of color faced. He made this statement after being instructed by Elijah Muhammad not to make any statements regarding the assassination. Malcolm was soon suspended from his role in the Nation.

Those within the Nation who were jealous of Malcolm took this opportunity to further assassinate Malcolm's character. However, the most defining factor of Malcolm's shift was the discovery of Elijah Muhammad's own immoral behavior of committing adultery with some of his former secretaries. Of course, Malcolm was completely crushed. Soon his association with the Nation of Islam would come to a complete end. Stepping out of the boundaries of the philosophy of the Nation, Malcolm emerged as a new political/social leader of the ghetto.

Minister James Shabazz, who was the minister of the temple in Newark, was assigned to Temple 7 as the interim minister until a minister could be chosen after Malcolm X left the Nation of Islam. Minister James's tenure as interim minister of Temple 7 was from the time of April or May of 1964 to May of 1965. During that time, ministers along the East Coast were rotated into the Newark Mosque on Sundays so that the spirit and the attendance of the Newark Mosque would not drop in the absence of its minister. Minister Shabazz was my minister also until he was murdered. He was an excellent teacher and leader. He had the nickname "Son of Thunder," but he was no Malcolm X.

Malcolm spelled out his new vision in his famous speech entitled "The Ballot or the Bullet."

> Malcolm began "The Ballot or the Bullet" speech by clarifying his religious status: "I'm still a Muslim," he said. "I still credit Mr. Muhammad for what I know and what I am." But in the interest of black unity, Malcolm stopped proselytizing or even discussing religion because of its propensity for creating divisions. While he was still deeply committed to Islam as the only true religion of blacks, his negative experiences in Muhammad's Black Muslim movement had shown him the limitations of religious fanaticism. As a consequence, Malcolm turned toward Martin Luther King as a model for the political direction in which he was now moving. . . .[3]

It has been forty-four long years since Malcolm X was murdered in February 1965. Arrested for this crime were five members of the Nation of Islam. However, many to this day, including myself, believe that the crime remains unsolved. Four of the arrested—Benjamin Thomas, Leon Davis, Wilbur McKinley, and William Bradley—have never been held accountable. Together with Talmadge Hayer (the only one of the original five to have served time for the crime), these individuals comprise what has been referred to as the Newark 5, a team of FOI that was established by the Nation of Islam's Newark Temple No. 25 to carry out the cold-blooded murder of Malcolm X. As my appreciation and respect for Malcolm grew, I started developing a dislike for being associated with the temple from whom the murders of Malcolm came.

I strongly believe that Malcolm was a man, like many of us, searching for the truth. My regret is that Malcolm and Martin never got the chance to communicate with each other on a level that would have allowed Martin to truly minister and witness to Malcolm through his life. Because of the level of commitment and the intelligence of Malcolm, it would have taken a Martin Luther King to bring Malcolm to the salvation of Jesus Christ, as I and many other former Muslims have experienced. In my own submission to the truth of Jesus Christ and the giving of honor to God's anointing, I was able to confess the error of my thinking and discussions. There were many times I spoke foolishly against Dr. King and the Christian faith in the name of Islam. After my conversion to Christianity and the born-again experience, I often would think with regret about some of the negative things I had said about this great man of God.

Knowing my heart, God arranged for the daughter of Dr. King, Bernice King, and me to be members of the same church. One Sunday, the Holy Spirit empowered me with the courage to do what I had wanted to do for a long time. I walked up to her, introduced myself, shared a little of my background, and apologized to her for my past actions. In my head I was thinking, *She thinks I'm crazy*, but in my spirit I was correcting a wrong I had committed against God's anointed servant Dr.

King and his daughter Bernice through Dr. King's direct bloodline. I recall her humble and gracious response followed by an embrace that released me from my own condemnation.

The death of Elijah Muhammad in 1975 was truly the death of the glory days of the Nation of Islam. First, there was the leadership split that arose when Elijah's son, Wallace D. Muhammad, took over the leadership. He changed the organization's name to the World Community of Islam in the West and sought to turn believers toward orthodox Islam. This was not received well by many members in the Nation, including Louis Farrakhan. He left from being under the leadership of W. D. Muhammad to continue teaching the doctrine of Elijah Muhammad under the organization's name, "Nation of Islam."

The breakup of the Nation of Islam under W. D. Muhammad's leadership proved that Elijah Muhammad was correct. He stated that blacks in the ghettos of America would not embrace orthodox Islamic teaching for the same reasons many were not truly embracing Christianity. He believed that neither religion directly addressed the identity, social and cultural problems the black community in America faced. Even I gradually started slipping away from my religious practices of prayer and fasting. Five

Chapter 4

When the Teacher Went
Back to School

IN STUDYING THE teachings and testimony of Malcolm X, I found the emotional and psychological support needed to allow myself to think outside of the box. This freedom was put to the test during a visit from my mother's cousin. I sometimes felt she would be boasting about the material things she had that my mother did not. I never liked it when she did it, but there was nothing I could do.

On this day, she was boasting about her daughter graduating from high school and going on to college. I will never forget the sadness that arose on my mother's face. I had never seen such a deep expression of it on her before. I thought to myself that this was something I could do something about. So I went back to school to get the "white man's education."

However, it was not going to be an easy process. Especially because I did not want my mother to know I was going back in case I failed. My journey back to school began with attending Central High night school. I would open the restaurant in the morning and go to school from 6 p.m. to 10 p.m. When my mother thought I was hanging out with my friends, I was sitting in a classroom. At times, I could not believe it. After completing my first year, I qualified to go back to regular school. When I got back to Barringer, I started slipping back into my old habits of just hanging out at the school or hooky parties.

By the grace of God, I was selected to apply to a new program the Newark Board of Education, Manpower, and the New Jersey Department of Education were launching. They built a brand-new school that focused on trades and occupational training. It was named Project COED, Center for Occupational Education and Development. The selection process included three interviews and an aptitude test. The test was to determine which course of study the students should take. I was accepted and placed into the Air Conditioning and Refrigeration class. In a short time, I fell in love with this school.

The program was structured for students to attend their regular high school in the morning and be bused to COED in the afternoon. The students were from schools all around the city. It was a first for me being in a school that included the poor and middle class, different races, and backgrounds. I felt so special being selected as a student in a brand-new school, with new books and equipment. As great as I found COED to be, it was not enough to help me my issues with regular school. Soon I was not even attending classes at Barringer anymore.

Making sure I would arrive with the other school buses, I would take public transportation to COED in the afternoon. This was working out well until about the middle of the second cycle. My counselor at COED, Ms. Higgins, called me into her office to question why my primary high school wanted to know why she was sending them my grades. As far as Barringer was concerned, I was not a student there. I had no choice but to explain and hope for the best. I was afraid I was going to be expelled from COED because the rules required students to attend both schools.

The day I was called to Ms. Higgins's office, the director of the school and the head counselor joined her. They confronted me about the situation, and I had no choice but to tell them the truth and hope for the best. They seemed to be amazed that I was a dropout "A" student at Barringer with a very good reputation at the school.

To be honest, a great deal of my motivation to study to get good grades was due to the wisdom of Ms. Higgins. She was the second school administrator I had a serious crush on. She used my infatuation to my advantage. She made an agreement with me that for every A or B grade I got on class assignments and tests, I could come help her in her office for an hour. That was the first time in my history as a student that I was pressing my teacher for extra assignments and projects.

Many times, I would be sitting in the class waiting for the teacher, Mr. Williams, to come in. Ms. Higgins was without a doubt my angel from God. She was the first to show interest in my future and back it up with action. She was the one who found and recommended an alternative school for me to attend and still be able to continue at COED. The school was called The Educational Center for Youth. It was a self-paced program, meaning I could complete classes at my own pace. It also allowed the students to graduate with a real high school diploma, not a GED, in the name of the last school they attended.

Because I could remain a student at COED, Ms. Higgins continued to be a major influence in my life. Once I was allowed to return to regular day school, I told my mother what I was doing to get my education. My mother loved Ms. Higgins and would even use her as leverage when she wanted me to do something I would buck about. Ms. Higgins even put the thought in my head that I was college material. She walked me through every single step of the college selection and application process. She coached me for my SAT test and even paid for a few of my college applications. Ms. Higgins understood the power of a woman and used it on me. She could have used my feelings for her for evil, but she used them for my good. For that, I will always be grateful to God for placing her in my life.

Because COED was a pilot school, the director handpicked a group of students to be representatives of the school and I was honored to be one of them. We would go to other high schools and talk to teachers and students about the program. We even made radio appearances on WBGO in Newark, New Jersey. A group of local and state politicians came to tour the school. My class and two other classes were asked to do a presentation based on what we were studying. Our project was an electronic board that demonstrated how a commercial air conditioning unit operated. We used actual parts on the board, like relays, transformers, and thermostats, and different colored lights on larger parts like motors and compressors. We impressed those visitors so much that the school was granted additional funding and received statewide attention.

At the end of that day, I received my first kiss on the cheek from Ms. Higgins. After that, I was writing politicians trying to get them to come to the school. I must admit it was a very proud moment for me.

Over the course of two years, I was able to catch up on my high school studies. By the grace of God, I actually pre-graduated (I completed my curriculum requirements in March) with a 3.7 grade point average and gave the graduation speech for my class. Looking out from the stage, I spotted my mother and Jenny, my friend who I met at COED. As I began to speak, Jenny placed her arms around by mother as the tears started to flow down her face. The pride, surprise, and tears that filled my mother's face that day were worth every hour of studying and sacrifice that I had to pay. I was able to experience the pleasure of seeing my mother's heart overflowing again, when the college acceptance letters started coming in. I must admit I was surprised myself. I never envisioned myself as a college student and only knew of one male from by community who had attended college.

My early completion of my high school requirements would turn out to be more of a blessing than I realized. It afforded me more time to work during my internship through COED. I was able to secure my internship at Prudential Insurance Co. in the building maintenance department. With a little more discipline under my belt, I saved my checks. My responsibilities included assisting with the maintenance and service of the air conditioning unit of the building.

Initially, I was completely overwhelmed with the size of the system and the amount of equipment and people required to operate it. This gave me a new respect and a view of opportunity for the air conditioning field. As I shared my experiences with Ms. Higgins, she suggested I consider studying mechanical engineering in college.

Now with a major in mind, Ms. Higgins and I began the college application process. To my surprise, I was accepted into several universities and colleges. My mother had recently come under doctor's care after being rushed to the hospital for high blood pressure. The doctors at the hopital also diagnosed her as having heart disease. Due to my mother's illness, I did not want to be too far from home. Therefore, I decided to enroll in New Jersey Institute of Technology to pursue a degree in mechanical engineering. Because NJIT did not offer the humanities classes required, I had to attend another school for my first two years. I chose Kean University to complete my first two years. I also chose Kean because the head counselor at COED had just started her new job as a counselor at Kean.

I never would have thought that I would have regrets about leaving school, but the day I graduated from COED, I was overwhelmed with mixed emotions. The truth is I was afraid to leave. Ms. Higgins and COED had provided me a place of safety, comfort, concern, support, encouragement, and hope. I was being celebrated for completing requirements that were causing me to be pushed out of the comfort of my nest. There was also a great deal of excitement about entering into a new world and flying on my own. I will forever be grateful to Ms. Higgins and to God for placing her in my life. If only our current educational system had more Ms. Higginses, we would have more success among African-American male high school students.

I don't think the impact of me actually going to college really hit me until my last night at home. As I started making rounds to some of my old neighborhoods to say goodbye before I was to report to the campus, I was greeted with shock, support (mainly from adults), and sadness. It was the support and sadness I felt from others that made me realize that this was not just about me.

The sadness I sensed from others was as if I had proven them wrong. Young black males could do it from our community and I had done it. The support and pride I felt from many parents made me feel as if I were representing them and their hope for their own sons. It was not a big deal to see the females from our community start this journey, but a male was a rare sight. I am sure if anyone had started a list of which of the males of our community would go on to college, I would have been on the very bottom of the list, if on it at all.

That morning my mom made a big breakfast. I was too excited to eat, but my brother made sure nothing was wasted. My mom had been doing anything she could do over the last few days up to this point. She kept apologizing for not having any money to give me. I had been saving my hustle money and my checks from my internship so I was okay.

As my brother and I loaded his car, he took a minute to talk to me about staying focused. He was the only one in our family to go to college before me. He attended Norfolk State on a football scholarship and a scholarship from NAACP. As he was starting his junior year, errors on his financial paperwork required him to sit out the first semester. While waiting to return, he was drafted into the military and served in the Vietnam war, never to return to college. I believe that is why his biggest concern for me was "Do what you need to do to finish. Nothing else matters."

Kean University

When we arrived at the campus, the three of us were impressed by how well- kept the campus grounds and buildings were. The most impressive thing happened after I got my dorm room assignment. The student dorms looked like four luxury high-rise apartment buildings with two buildings facing each other and in the middle was a park-like area surrounded by a circular driveway. The dorm buildings had an apartment floor plan. Each apartment had a kitchen, eating area, living room, two bedrooms, and a bathroom. It was nothing like other dorms I had seen. My brother joked about kicking my roommates out and coming to stay with me.

Before leaving me at the school, my mom gave me a big hug with tears in her eyes from mixed emotions. She was so proud of me, but she kept apologizing for not being able to do more for me. I think she noticed some of the things other students were bringing and being given credit cards. That really did not bother me because I was a hustler and I was just amazed to be there.

However, when my brother pulled out a knot of cash to give me, that made my mom and me feel even better. I think that's when my big brother really became my hero. Not just because he gave me money, he had done that before. This time I felt he was saying he believed in me.

The most interesting thing about that first day of college that I recall and often think about to this day was the instant transformation of many of the summer freshmen as soon as their parents left. I was a little intimidated; this was my first time ever being around that many white students. As I moved among these students, they seemed so in control, confident, and well mannered.

However, as soon as their parents were out of sight, there was an instant shift to wild and reckless, especially the females. I thought, *I just witnessed an Academy Award-winning performance.* Then it began to settle in my mind that as a person I was not less than they were, but I just was not as good a performer.

My freshman year at Kean was one of the most exciting years of my life. I was used to the whole "disco" scene, but college parties were on a whole other level. The rooms would be so packed the walls would be sweating and the windows so fogged up you could not see. Every time campus police would come to break up the party, we would just break up into several smaller groups and let P-Funk rule the night. Because of my involvement at COED with political and social clubs, I immediately was involved in student government and won the office of freshman class president. This empowered me to do absolutely nothing but sit in on the Student Council meetings and be the voice of the freshmen. This meant I really did not have much of a voice at all. The last thing on the minds of most freshmen was student government. It did allow me to get the attention of one of the major council members, who was the president of the black student union.

Chris was a real mover and shaker on campus. He was involved in everything, very intelligent, and the first student I met who was completely focused on his education and future. Chris was in his senior year and was looking for someone to replace him as president of the Black Student Union. He said that after he had watched me in the meetings, I was his choice. I don't know when this guy slept. Along with taking classes, student government functions, and mentoring me, he was also the campus president of Omega Psi Phi fraternity, also known as "the Qs."

Of course, this was the fraternity he was guiding me to become a member of. I grew impressed with what they said they stood for. I was really impressed to learn that Bill Cosby was a member. That was the biggest selling point for me. With Chris's help, before I knew it I was "online." Being "online" means that an individual is being considered to becoming a member. For a number of weeks the individual would be required to various tasks and activities to to demonstrate their worthiness to be a member of the fraternity. The term "online" may have been coined from the fact that everyone attempting to join the fraternity had to travel around campus as a group and walk in a straight line.

At this time, I was the new president of the Black Student Union. I was the first sophomore to hold the position. I had invitations from every black fraternity on campus to join their line that semester. Later I came to understand why. It was not so much me they wanted but the favor I would bring with me as the president of the BSU.

After a few weeks, the issues that accompanied being on line began to trouble me. Much of it had to do with my personal beliefs and opinions developed as a member of the Nation of Islam. For example, I could not understand why the "pledging" process had to be so violent, degrading, and humiliating.

The breaking point for me was when others and I stepped in to assist one of our line brothers being beaten by frat members from another school. This turned into a big fight and big issue on campus. I had to address the issue with school staff and students as leader of the African-American students, not a pledgee. As such, I expressed my anger, embarrassment, and disappointment in the lack of support our own campus members had provided. These actions also seemed to contradict one of the major selling points for me in my decision to join, which was the upholding of black pride, manhood, and unity. After that, I decided it would be best for me to drop off line.

As president of the BSU, my greatest challenge was overcoming my fear of being ill prepared for the position. The manifestation of that fear came when I learned the amount of the budget we had to work with thanks to Chris, who had fought and negotiated for the budget the year before.

The most money I had had control of at one time was several hundred dollars. Most times I blew that. Now here I was with control of over eleven thousand dollars. That was a lot of money for someone nineteen years old in 1978. More than just the amount of money concerned me—my mentors made it very clear to me that how I spent that money would determine how much would be awarded the following year.

Much of the budget in place was earmarked for entertainment. With the charge that had been given to me in mind, I began seeking ways to balance the spending between entertainment, education, and social issues. We still had plenty of parties and a major concert with Gil Scott Herring, a trip to Cherry Hill, New Jersey, to see Patti Label, and a camping trip to Bear Mountain, Pennsylvania. That trip was mainly for others like me who did not have much opportunity to venture outside of the inner city much. That trip still remains one of my fondest memories of college.

In addition, we were able to invite in some of the most influential speakers of that time, including Dr. Na'im Akbar who spoke on the subject of breaking the chain of psychological slavery. The position of president of the Black Student Union did what all of the African history books I read could not do. I was proud to be me. It also helped re-direct my studies. After taking a political science and pre-law course, I decided to pursue a career as an attorney.

At Kean, I also met some really good friends. Two of those good friends were Derrick and Kim. Kim was very special because she was the first girlfriend I had who, after we broke up, we became truly best friends to each other. We were so close that others we dated would get upset. Many accused us of sleeping together, but we were just close friends. We trusted each other with our fears, secrets, everything.

We both were in love with New York. On the weekends when she went home to South Jersey to see her mother, we would take the train to New York and hang out in Washington Square Park or Central Park. We would always talk about our plans of becoming successful and moving to Manhattan. We both moved to New York. Kim graduated, got a job as a teacher, and settled in Brooklyn. I made it to Manhattan, but not the way we talked about it. My westside apartment was not the result of my hard work as an attorney, but of my hustle as a drug dealer.

Rutgers University

In my junior year of college, I transferred to Rutgers University, Newark Campus. I transferred for several reasons. First, Rutgers was a better school in terms of academic credibility. Also my mother began to become ill due to high blood pressure, so I wanted to be closer to her.

I knew my transfer to Rutgers would demand a change and place a greater challenge on my study habits, but I was excited about being there. I lost some credits in the transfer, but it was worth it. I decided to major in Criminal Justice/Pre-Law and minor in Marketing. When I told my mother that I had decided I wanted to be a lawyer, she thought that was a good idea and I would make a good lawyer because I was a good liar. Not quite the compliment I was looking for, but I took it.

It was at Rutgers that I received the mis-education that smoking marijuana helped me study. Before then, I mostly enjoyed it while dancing or listening to music. I really thought that I would read, study, write, and take tests better when I was high. Between schoolwork, music, and dancing, it was simply the grace of God that I remembered anything. I was a member of the Pre-Law Club. When we had debates or mock trials, you could walk in the class and the smell of marijuana just slapped you in the face.

During one of our Pre-Law forums, we had the first African-American female presiding judge in Newark as a guest speaker. Her speech excited me more about a career in law. Afterward I introduced myself to her and she offered to assist and advise me.

At this time, finances at home started getting tighter on my mother. So I decided to take a leave from Rutgers to attend a paralegal school that had a one-year program. My plan was to graduate, get a job as a paralegal, and go back to Rutgers at night. This way I could help my mother, actually start my legal career, and still pursue attending law school. However, as we all know, things rarely work out the way we plan them, at least for me. Two weeks after I graduated and received my paralegal diploma, my mother passed away.

Chapter 5

The Year to Remember

MY GIRLFRIEND, GENNIE, was home for the summer. She attended Rutgers in Livingston, New Jersey. Once again, she was sitting beside my mother, witnessing me graduate. This time it was not a high school diploma, but a Paralegal diploma. As I looked at them in the audience, I was so happy that I had given them something else to be proud of, another unexpected victory and achievement in my life.

Several weeks after my graduation, Gennie and I had just come back to my house from a bike ride. My mother started complaining that she was hot. This was unusual for my mom. I never recalled my mom complain about the heat before. Gennie and I left to go around the corner to get her some ice cream from the parlor.

When we returned, we found her on the floor struggling to breathe. I told Gennie to go to the fire station, which was at the corner of our block, for help. I tried to give her mouth-to-mouth to revive her when I noticed she had slipped away. But I was unable to bring her back to consciousness. The medics from the fire department worked on her until the ambulance came. As we were heading for the hospital, I felt moved to just wrap my arms around her. That was the last time I was able to do so. We believe at that moment my mom passed away in my arms.

My greatest regret was that I was not able to take care of my mom as I had promised I would. I felt it was her time to enjoy life. Honestly, I was angry that God felt otherwise. For me, the very concept of being angry with God was unheard of. I dared not express this anger, so I did what I knew how to do best—I bottled it up. Little did I know that very soon I would be the target of that same anger I was directing towards God. If only I had understood the value of forgiveness then, as I do now, my life would have been completely different.

It appeared that everything I valued most about family life that we operated in also died with my mother. She was the chief cornerstone and the glue of the family that kept us standing and connected. The one solid connection that remained for me was my relationship with my brother, Mustafa.

My brother had changed his birth name from Jesse Reddick, Jr., to Mustafa Muhammad soon after he returned home from Vietnam and joined the Nation of Islam. Mustafa was ten years older than I was. Because of that, we were not that close growing up, but I always admired him. He was a local sport superstar at Central High School in Newark, New Jersey, where he participated in track, basketball, and football. He was respected and well liked in the community.

Often when I would get in a situation in the community (which translates fighting or some other trouble), someone would mention "that's Jesse little brother" and the situation would change. Those times always made me feel special.

Mustafa was accepted to Virginia State on a football scholarship and he received a scholarship from UNCF (United Negro College Fund). He had already been invited to attend the New York Giants camp. During his third year, there was a mix up with his scholarship funds from UNCF and this caused him to be unable to enroll as a student. It was during this time that he was drafted into the military and deployed in Vietnam.

When my brother was in Vietnam, he would write and send pictures and gifts to my mom and me often. I remember that he sent me a green army jacket with different patches on it and the words "Vietnam Saigon" stitched on the back. I wore that jacket so much my mom had to take it from me in the summer.

It was when my brother returned home that we became very close. At various times he was my brother, my father, and my best friend. My fondest memories are of our Saturday bike rides through New York. We would ride all day from Battery Park, over the Brooklyn Bridge, Central Park, and into Harlem. We both loved going into Harlem. I felt a sense of being connected to African American history there. I also loved our train rides. He worked for Amtrak as an ironworker, so we were able to ride anywhere for free.

Soon after my mother died, I began selling drugs. Like many other individuals who started down the road of selling drugs, my drug dealing venture was only suppose to last until I reached a monetary goal I had set. That goal was to save enough money for a down payment for a house and some money for law school.

My girlfriend at the time was pregnant with our first daughter. I did not want to buy a house in Newark. I was attracted to an area in South Orange, New Jersey. It was in the neighborhood surrounding Seton Hall University. They were the closest I had seen that compared to ones portrayed on television programs and movies. I was talking about simple things like grass, trees, clean streets, driveways, and backyards with swing sets. I wanted that for my unborn daughter and I thought selling drugs was the quickest way to get me there.

The drug business was slow moving at first. I didn't know anyone to "teach me the game." I started out by finding an unclaimed corner on South Orange Avenue in the Vailsburg section of Newark. I would go out at night after work until one of my customers asked me to let her son work for me and I did. I then moved to another location and started selling there.

Things were still slow moving until I met my new cocaine connection through a friend. We met at a dance club I was a member of in New York called Paradise Garage. My new connection provided me with better product at lower cost and more important, as we became closer, I was mentored into the business. In a matter of months, I moved off the corner to selling out of three apartments, one in the Bronx and two in Newark.

In addition, I used my connections as a court clerk to develop more upscale group customers, who included attorneys, stockbrokers, executives, etc. I also used this position to sell drugs to inmates who were in pre-trial holding through two court officers I recruited. The money was coming so quickly it actually scared me for a moment. With mentoring, I became good and successful in what I did. When it came to testing, cutting, and cooking (preparing it to be smoked), I was known as "the kitchen chemist." I was getting paid to show others how to cook. This was before "crack." Then it was known as "freebasing."

When cocaine base started being sold at street level, it became known as "crack." This name stems from the sound the processed cocaine makes when it is smoked. It made a cracking sound because it was cooked using baking soda, which was cheaper, less dangerous, and easier to get than ether but not as effective. Crack not only opened the floodgates for profits, but also for demonic bondage and addiction.

When I had the money I started out to get, I still stayed in the game. I didn't understand why at the time. It was not until I learned about the nature of addiction that I understood I had become addicted to the lifestyle. The fast money, power, excitement, danger, sex, and for me, being able to help others financially, kept me in the game.

My brother wanted to come stay at my place overnight for a cool down period. At the time I had a business transaction at my place so I asked if he could give me a few hours before coming over. I didn't want my family to know that I was selling drugs, especially my brother. My job as a court clerk served as a good cover.

My brother went to the home of a longtime friend of ours, who we referred to as our cousin. He was also involved in drugs and other things. One of his enemies had a contract to kill him. They came to his home the night I sent my brother there and killed everyone in the house, including my brother. The children survived because their mother hid them in the closet upstairs before she was murdered. My brother would not have been there if I was not so caught up in the game. All the times he had been there for me when I needed something and the one time my brother asked for a simple favor of spending the night at my apartment, I put him off. This is why I blamed myself for his murder.

I could not deal with the guilt, shame, and self-condemnation, so I began free-falling away from the pain with the help of smoking cocaine. I acted as police, prosecutor, judge, and prison warden as I sentenced myself to the prison of drug addiction and the beginning of my life becoming a living hell on earth.

Chapter 6

From Court Clerk to Inmate

AFTER EARNING MY Paralegal diploma, I returned to Rutgers University to continue my studies of Criminal Justice/Pre-Law. My desire was to attend law school with a focus on corporate law. It was at this time I tested, interviewed for, and was offered a position as court docket clerk in Newark, New Jersey. Within six months, I was promoted to the court clerk position. I was informed that I was the youngest African-American male to hold that position. I believe I was twenty-one years old.

A team of six of us reported directly to the presiding judge. She also issued the courtroom assignments and which judges we were to assist. Because I enjoyed doing legal research I quickly became the "judge's pet." I honestly think it was because my approach to the job was completely different. I did not see my work as a means to a weekly paycheck, but as an opportunity to gain mentors, allies, and recommendations to assist in my acceptance to law school.

I was working my plan and things seem to be moving in the direction of my goal until the news came that Gina, my girlfriend, was pregnant. This was not my first time in this position. Gennie had been pregnant with my child twice during the four years we dated. Both times we decided to abort. Both times I felt like s***, but we were young and scared. We were so focused on getting out of the ghetto that there simply was no room for a child.

When Gina shared the news with me about her desire to have our child, I quickly agreed. I started making adjustments to my plans. Those adjustments included additional income. That additional income would come from the drug business I would soon start.

I started thinking about the environment I grew up in and I wanted my first child to have better. Although Gina kept trying to assure me all would be fine (I had a great-paying job and a career ahead of me), that was not enough for me. I started selling small bags of marijuana. I quickly moved up to ounces, but this was too slow and transportation was too risky.

I was a member of an exclusive dance club called the Paradise Garage in New York. I was there every single weekend. From Friday night to Sunday afternoon, that is where I could be found. I started helping with security at the club. It was at the club that I made my cocaine connection. We quickly transitioned from a buyer/seller relationship to a mentor-friend/mentee-friend relationship. I was a great student and learned the drug business quickly. Things began moving so fast I felt as if I was just going along for the ride. It was becoming more difficult to hide what I was doing from my family.

It was in an attempt to keep my drug dealing from my family that I delayed a request of my brother to visit with me—because of a drug deal. My decision to go forward with the deal and delay a visit with my brother cost him his life.

My original intent for going into this business was to save enough money for a good down payment for a house for my girlfriend and our child and some finances for law school. The fast money and excitement caused me to lose sight of those original intentions. The truth is that I just got greedy. My weekly paycheck and drug dealing income just was not enough (even though it truly was), so I developed another money-generating venture.

Part of my duty as a court clerk was to record all court proceedings. I was also in charge of the courtroom when the judge was not on the bench. This included the supervision of the court interpreter, court officers, and court interviewers. My plan was simple. Whenever I was assigned to clerk in arraignment court, I would change the bails the judge would issue once he left the bench for a fee I would charge the defendants. I would pay my court interviewer to locate a possible "client." This was natural for him because his job was to interview the family members to determine what assisted they may or may not need. For example, if they needed a bailbondsman, public defender, medical assistance, etc. I only dealt with drug dealing offenses because I knew the defendants have access to cash. This afforded me the opportunity. Once the interviewer was locate someone interested in the offer to "help" them with the bail, we would negotiate in "new" bond and my fee amount. I would then change the bail bond order and forward it to the holding cell and clerk's office. The family would then pay the bail I set and the defendant would be released.

The money was good, but I think I was more addicted to the power and excitement of it all. I also believe that is what led to my downfall. One day I noticed a young Hispanic woman and her mother sitting in court. Both were crying non-stop. The young woman's father had been arrested for a "low-volume attempt to distribute" charge. Meaning he was selling five- to fifty-dollar packages of drugs. He was a street corner dealer. Because the woman was attractive and I truly felt for them, I decided to help. I changed her father's bail to a signature bond (this allowed him to sign himself out). They had no real money so I only charged them enough to pay the interviewer something to keep him quiet.

This happened in the morning, so as I was leaving for the day I noticed the two ladies still sitting in the lobby. I checked to see what the hold-up was and learned that the father's paperwork had been misplaced. I told the two women what had happened and that he would be released soon. Well, they did not believe me and reported me.

The following morning, I was summoned to the presiding judge's office. That was not uncommon because she would call me in for assignment changes or to discuss how I was doing in school. As I walked into her office with a cup of Cuban coffee in hand, I noticed the district attorney sitting in the office and the water in her eyes. They were tears of extreme disappointment. As I was taking my seat, the presiding judge pointed behind me and asked if I knew the individuals who were seated behind her office door. As I turned and saw who it was, I placed my coffee on her desk as my hands began to shake uncontrollability.

As I looked at the two women, the daughter mouthed the words "I'm sorry." When the women saw me leaving work, they thought that I had cheated them out of their money and reported me. As they walked out of the office after reporting me, the father was standing on steps outside, looking for them.

Because this happened during an election year, my crime turned into a political firestorm. The presiding judge and I agreed to help each other. I felt I owed her that much, plus I didn't have much of a choice. The agreement was to reveal my arrest in a news release as the result of an ongoing investigation of her office into corruption in the court system. I had to explain how I did what I did without it being detected, who was involved with me, and I identified all the defendants whose bail I had changed. By the time the investigation was over, I was charged with sixty-seven counts of official misconduct, obstruction of justice, and conspiracy. In return for my cooperation, I would be given a reduced sentence.

One of my ways of escape from what could have been decades of prison time came out of a belief that was actually insulting and racist. So much so that my pride and ego almost cost me my freedom. The lead investigator for the Essex County District Attorney's office said to me, "There was no way you came up with this plan." I need to give them the "mastermind" in order for them to honor any deal. Honestly, I don't know if it was because I was young or African-American or both, but he was not going to believe this was my doing and planning. I gave them the name of a court officer I did not like—he was older, white, but had absolutely nothing to do with it. I knew he would be cleared of the charges because they had no proof other than my statement.

When the time came for me to receive my sentencing, the court was packed with the media and it looked like the prosecutor had left me in the hands of the judge. My charges were reduced to one count each and I was sentence to nine years. One week later I returned in front of the same judge. This time, it was late in the afternoon with no media or spectators. I was re-sentenced to one year. Because I had obtained employment at J. C. Penney as a buyer's assistant, I was placed on the weekend program. I reported in on Friday evenings and signed out on Sundays. I served about three months before what remain on my sentence was suspended.

Chapter 7

Introduction to Freebase

NEAR THE HEIGHT of my drug dealing business, I was escorted to a place that appeared to be paradise but was revealed as my hell on earth. It started out as a normal night of business in a studio apartment on west side of Central Park in Manhattan. This was a safe place to meet, transact business, and relax. What made this night different was the presence of three beautiful women and my foolish pride and ego.

Katy was one of my supplier's girlfriends. She was a beautiful, tall, Australian party girl. She was not around much because she worked as a flight attendant for a major airline. When she was in town, you could not miss her in the clubs.

Katy and one of her friends were at the apartment. We were doing cocaine lines, smoking reefer, and listening to music. Katy and her friend disappeared in the kitchen. I was not aware of what they were doing, but my supplier was. He received a phone call and had to leave for a few hours. Before he walked out, he warned me several times to stay out of the kitchen and not to get involved with what they were doing. Of course, that just made me more interested. Soon after he left, I made my way into the kitchen. What I saw amazed me. Katy and her friend were freebasing.

Freebasing is a form of using cocaine by smoking it. Powder cocaine can be smoked but it is a less effective method. Freebasing was a form of use that I was completely unfamiliar with. All I knew was that high-rolling celebs on the West Coast were doing it. The process was to treat cocaine with ether or other chemicals, which freed the cocaine base from the other chemicals used to "cut" the cocaine. The mixture would then be heated up until the cocaine was melted into oil. The oil base was separated and quickly chilled down until it was hardened again. This enabled the cocaine base, which would now be pure cocaine, to be easily smoked. Cocaine treated in this way is known as "freebase."

Although my friend had told me to stay away, I was too interested in what they were doing. When Katy offered me some, I first said no. If I knew then what I know now, I would have run out of the apartment and left them there. But I stayed and watched them. The second time her friend offered me to try some. This time she used the magic words men often fall victim to. She asked, "Are you scared?"

In my defense, I was a twenty-three-year-old black man walking around with at least a thousand dollars in my pocket every day, feeding into the possibility of being the next Nicky Barnes. In my mind I had arrived and I could not let two white girls punk me out. So I played the fool on my own accord. I knew I was hooked after the first hit because it scared me, but a few minutes later I asked for more.

I think the major addictive factor for me was the emotional numbing effect of freebasing. Of all the other illegal drugs that I had used, freebasing takes effect within seconds of being inhaled. It is a very efficient way of delivering cocaine to the brain in a matter of seconds. There is an initial rush of immensely pleasurable feelings lasting for up to two minutes, followed by an intense high lasting for about thirty minutes. This provided me with a high that completely erased all my emotional pain.

At first, I had to rely on Katy to transform the cocaine powder to its base form (a process known as "cooking") when she was in town. As I progressed in my addiction, relying on Katy to "cook" for me was becoming less acceptable so I paid her to teach me. I learned several different ways of cooking. The best results, which came from cooking the cocaine powder down to its purest form, were obtained by using ether. But this was also the most dangerous. The quickest and safer way was to use baking soda. When mass-producing freebase (or crack), we used microwave ovens for the heat source.

In the eighties, freebasing became popular in New York and New Jersey. From the business end, this form of using cocaine was a dream come true. Because it was powerfully and quickly addictive, it equaled the demand for powered cocaine. In some areas, it took over.

At first it was expensive to freebase. To make it worthwhile you had to buy at least $100 to $250 worth of rock cocaine. This was equal to 1 to 3.5 grams of cocaine. However, the use of baking soda made it easy for dealers to cook the cocaine themselves and sell it on the street for as little as $3. Those who did not know how to cook or do it well would hire "cookers." This was a line of revenue to tap into. I had become very good at cooking. My peers in the business gave me the title of Kitchen Chemist. The sad part about that was that I really was proud of the title.

This cheap form of basing in the street had spread like wildfire. On the streets, it was known as "crack rock" or "crack." People who freebased were called "baseheads." We had our own culture. We cooked our own cocaine; we used expensive glass bowls and pipes to smoke out of, using a mini torch. We used torches because of the intensity of the heat, which quickly caused the base rock to smoke before turning to oil and running away from the heat. This was important because the more smoke you could develop, the better it would be. After all of the base cocaine was smoked, we would then smoke the oil.

This was done in two ways: one was to heat the bottom of the glass pipe and cause the oil to burn and smoke. This was dangerous because many times the pipes would explode from the heat if you did not heat it right. Or we would put rubbing or grain alcohol into the bowl. This removed the oil from the glass and mixed it with the alcohol. We then poured the alcohol mixture out of the pipe onto a mirror. Then we ignited the alcohol. The fire burned away the alcohol and left cocaine oil. Let it dry, scrape it up with a razor blade, put it in your pipe, and smoke it just like the original rock. Some of us referred to this as resurrecting the base. (Ain't that something!?)

The thing with crack is that because of how dealers cook it and what they may mix with it, the "high" is not as powerful or lasting. Therefore, you smoke it quicker, leaving the user feeling agitated and needing another hit to feel better. That is the hook of the addiction and the joy of the dealer. Crack gets its name because when smoked, the baking soda residue left in it crackles. However, the more it crackles is an indication that it was not cooked right. But those who did not know any better thought that meant it was good.

I believe one of the most misunderstood factors of being addicted to smoking crack is the fact that many become addicted to the process of smoking almost as much as they are to smoking itself. The physical, mental, and psychological processes of smoking cocaine can be very similar to going through religious rituals. Every action adds to the whole experience. From looking at the number or size of the rocks in your hands to watching the smoke build up and flow through the pipe into your mouth. At that point, absolutely nothing else mattered to me. A selfishness consumed me, the likes of which I never want to operate in again.

I know that those in the medical profession refer to crack addiction as a disease. I see it more as a demonic stronghold. I have used many kinds and types of illegal drugs in my life. None of those affected my life and my soul with the darkness that smoking cocaine did. This drug use affected my body and soul.

I have been delivered from this demonic oppression for twenty years now and counting. Yet I still occasionally have what is referred to as cocaine dreams (dreaming about using the drug). What is interesting, to which my wife will bear witness, is that whenever the processes of using in my dreams come, I never just accept them. I fight them in my sleep and I wake up having decided not to use it in my dream.

This is why I praise God and proclaim the name of Jesus the way I do. Why I cry when I think about His kindness, grace, mercy, and compassion toward me. I thank Him because by His blood and the indwelling of the Holy Spirit, weapons of mass destruction may form, but they have not and will not prosper.

Today, I thank God for common sense. There were times I did not have the sense of a pig. Why do I say this? Let us take a ride and look at some uncommon situations that lead us to witnessing the sense of a pig.

Mark 5:2-13 records the following:

And when he was come out of the ship, immediately there met him out of the tombs a man with an unclean spirit, Who had his dwelling among the tombs; and no man could bind him, no, not with chains: Because that he had been often bound with fetters and chains, and the chains had been plucked asunder by him, and the fetters broken in pieces: neither could any man tame him. And always, night and day, he was in the mountains, and in the tombs, crying, and cutting himself with stones. But when he saw Jesus afar off, he ran and worshipped him, And cried with a loud voice, and said, What have I to do with thee, Jesus, thou Son of the most high God? I adjure thee by God, that thou torment me not. For he said unto him, Come out of the man, thou unclean spirit. And he asked him, What is thy name? And he answered, saying, My name is Legion: for we are many. And he besought him much that he would not send them away out of the country. Now there was there nigh unto the mountains a great herd of swine feeding. And all the devils besought him, saying, Send us into the swine, that we may enter into them. And forthwith Jesus gave them leave. And the unclean spirits went out, and entered into the swine: and the herd ran violently down a steep place into the sea, (they were about two thousand;) and were choked in the sea.

Our first stop in this text is an uncommon place. This area was located in one of several cities that were known as "the Decapolis." Among these cities was the countryside. This was a location of tombs and graves where the dead were placed and other living outcasts of society dwelled there. The location, with its tombs, was a great hiding place for criminals, the poor, and the insane. Like our inner cities, it was a dead environment and a burial site of thousands of dreams, visions, ideals, and hopes. It contained stockpiles of unused and untapped gifts and abilities. A place from which where few are able to escape.

What made it uncommon for Jesus to show up at this place was that it was mostly a Gentile region. At this time, His assignment was toward the Jews. The "whosoever shall" of John 3:15-16 was a timeless truth. But the appointed time for the outreach to the Gentiles had not yet come.

Now let's ride to an uncommon condition. The text states that this man meets Jesus and immediately falls down and worships Him. This man's condition consisted of having more than one "unclean spirit," yet he worshipped Jesus.

The Greek word translated "worship" here means "to express by attitude and possibly by position one's allegiance to and regard for deity." So this worship by Legion was simply a function of common sense. The sounding alarm here is that demons seem to have more common sense than we whom God calls His highest creation.

I see this in the lack of respect, homage, and honor we give to the Word of God, the house of God, and the men and women of God. It appears that we have lost the common sense that tells us to operate in reverence to whom or what God has His hands on. I hear Christians, so quick to give opinions and judgment, yet slow, if ever, to pray, intercede, and restore, as we are instructed to do. What about the message this communicates to others?

This man's condition was such that no one could bind him. His family and friends made attempts to help him with tough love, self-help programs, hospitals, and even religion. All hope of helping him was abandoned. So this man was left to deal with himself alone. There was a time in my life where this was the most frightening place to be, alone with myself. At opportune times I would do anything—have television, CDs, or the radio playing as loud as possible, just so I could not be alone with my thoughts and memories.

Out of the man's agony, he would cut himself with stones. I can honestly relate to such self-inflicting pain. I walked the streets many nights, crying from the pain of cutting myself with stones of self-condemnation, self-hatred, and self-torment. Crying out because deep inside I knew my current situation was not meant to be my final destination, but I did not know how to make the transition. I was in an uncommon place with an uncommon call upon my life, whose fulfillment required uncommon reaction. Here I want to introduce you to the pigs.

Pigs are characterized as being greedy, unclean, stubborn, and even unhealthy creatures. In the book of Second Peter, false teachers are compared to dogs and pigs (see 2 Peter 2:22). The pig became a symbol for baseness, paganism, and uncleanness.

Contrary to popular belief, pigs do not play in the mud simply because they are filthily. They are unable to sweat so they wallow in mud to cool down.

Many people think of them as stupid. I did too until I watched a nature program entitled "The Joy of Pigs." The show revealed how intelligent pigs really are. They are smarter than any other domestic animal and have one of the highest abilities among animals to solve problems. They are more trainable than dogs or cats. To scientists, pigs are unusual because they are one of the only large mammals that exist, in one form or another, in every part of the world.

With this information as a backdrop, let's look at this reaction. Jesus gave the demons authority to enter the pigs, but the pigs refused to give them power to operate through them. Could the pigs have been intelligent enough to know the demons had no power to operate through them? If so, then the demons were sensed (perceived and understood to be evil), rejected. and resisted by these pigs to the point of death. They had enough sense to deliver themselves by an act of death.

This was not an act of suicide by the pigs or murder at the hands of the demons. The demons needed the bodies of the pigs for them to stay in that region, so why would they cause the pigs to commit suicide? The answer is they would not.

We have all at some point in our lives found ourselves in unusual, strange, or unattractive places and spaces. We have been in locations we easily entered into, but were completely lost in finding the way out. It is the uncommon events, conditions, and reactions of human life that direct us to a common reality, through the application of common sense. That common reality is sin. It has already been declared, "all have sinned and come short of the glory of God" (John 3:15-16).

Common sense can help keep you from evil bondage. Proverbs 3:21-23 instructs us to "guard clear thinking and common sense with your life; don't for a minute lose sight of them. They'll keep your soul alive and well, they'll keep you fit and attractive."[4]

Could the pigs have been intelligent and sensible enough to sense, perceive, and understand these demons were evil? Could they sense that the demons had no right to possess them? Therefore, they were rejected and resisted by these pigs to the point of death. If there is something you sense in your life that is not pleasing to God, yet you are unwilling to die to it, then you have allowed the pigs in biblical account to operate with honor and wisdom greater than yours. I believe they killed themselves because of the sense of evil they felt after the demons entered them, not because the demons make them do it. The demons wanted them to live, not die. That's why the demons asked Jesus to allow them to go into the pigs.

Chapter 8

The First Breaking Point

DECEMBER 30, 1989, started as just another Saturday for me. I met the day planning, thinking, and scheming about getting my high for the day. By this time my drug dealing business had collapsed due to me being my best customer. I was using more than I was selling. I was unemployed and homeless. I stayed in various crack houses that were run by former associates of mine.

I also did collections and drop-offs for a former supplier. It bothered him to see how low and lost I was. He didn't show or express it, but I knew it. He allowed me to do various jobs for him in an attempt keep me from doing other things to get high. He often paid me with cocaine because he knew I would just go somewhere else and buy it. I understand completely now that the favor I had with my supplier was provided by God to keep me until I came to Him. The things my supplier did for me, gave me, and looked the other way about was unheard of for him. When it came to business, he was no nonsense.

Sometimes I would sell some to get a room for the night and some food. Many times, I would smoke it all up and eat by doing what is known in the homeless world as "dumpster dives." I would wait until around closing time and jump inside various dumpsters behind fast food restaurants to get leftover food they were throwing away. At some places, I would just go in and ask for it.

As bad as I was, I still had my limits. One of them was to do whatever was necessary to keep from robbing people in the street. I have seen a lot of violence in my life. I remember reading a newspaper article years ago stating that the amount of street violence that youth in the urban areas of New York and New Jersey were exposed to in a three-year period was equal to what a Vietnam combat soldier would have witnessed. I had witnessed and been a part of my share. So when those situations came up that required a violent response, I often would get coked up to shift my mind to a place that would allow me to act accordingly. But what I would have to witness that night, no amount of cocaine could have helped.

I was asked that night to accompany three other workers for my former supplier on a collection run. Theses "collection runs" were the outcomes of not paying your debt. I really did not like doing these often because they were very draining emotionally and physically. Often my assignments on these runs were to scout the area, provide cover, and be a lookout. This run took us into an apartment building in Spanish Harlem. What made this more uncomfortable for me was the feeling that I stood out. Spanish Harlem was a mixed community of Spanish speaking people, mainly Puerto Ricans.

The person we were looking for was a low-level street dealer who had gotten in over his head. We found him and I pretended to want to buy an "eight ball." An eight ball was three and a half grams of crack cocaine that would sell for $225 to $275. I told him I might want more. He took me to the building where we knew he lived and told me to wait out front. He returned with the crack and told me to smoke a piece of crack in front of him. This made him more comfortable that I was not a cop. I took the rock from him and acted like I dropped it putting it the pipe. That's when my three associates came and grabbed him. He swore he had the money upstairs in his apartment. When we entered his apartment we found a woman and a baby. This made me very uncomfortable and soon my biggest fears came true. He did not have all the money.

Immediately, guns were pulled and one of the three guys quickly grabbed the baby from the woman. He took the baby, holding it by one ankle, to the small balcony and held it over the railing. This is when we learned the woman was his girlfriend and the baby was his child. I was completely on edge. This was out of my style of dealing with people. But I could not say anything that would display any sign of fear or weakness. I used the girlfriend's initial scream when the baby was taken from her as an excuse to check the hallway. The truth was, I just could not witness any more of what was happening and what I was afraid would happen next.

The door to the apartment opened and my three associates and the dealer came out. We took him to his car, a late model black and red Mustang. Two of my associates got in the car with him. We followed them to one of the crack spots my supplier operated. I knew this meant they were about to really beat this guy up bad. They told me they had it from there and paid me. I did not waste any time getting out of there. I jumped on the train to Manhattan. I was on my way to Newark, but I decided not to go. I had enough of living like this.

I rented a cheap hotel room off Eighth Avenue and Forty-Fourth Street in Manhattan. The place was a dump and was primarily used by prostitutes working the streets. I had brought an "eight ball" (three and a half grams) of crack cocaine, a new pipe, and a torch. A torch was a mini torch-like lighter that was used to smoke cocaine with because of the intense heat it provide to quickly burn the cocaine to produce smoke before it melted away. I took my first hit as I would normally do and enjoyed momentary escape. For my second hit, I packed the bowl of the pipe with as much cocaine as I could. I heated the stem so that the oil that would run from the bowl under the stem would begin to turn to smoke. This way I would get much smoke into my lungs as possible. For this hit, my goal was to get not just a momentary escape from my life, but a permanent one. This was my cowardly attempt to commit suicide.

I say cowardly because I was afraid of the outcome of having killed myself. In my warped thinking, I believed a drug overdose would have been better than shooting myself in the head or cutting my wrist. I had been taught that suicide was against the will of God and I would go to hell if I did so. But at this point I could see no other way out. So I took the hit and hoped for God's understanding and forgiveness. I took the hit and passed out.

When I regained consciousness, I was lying on the floor with my pipe broken next to me and the torch still in my hand. It was still on but had burned out. I did not think about this until months later, but not only did my heart not explode as I had planned; I had no explanation as to why that cheap carpet in the room did not catch on fire through the torch that was burning in my hand. I clearly understand now that it was another moment of God's grace in my life.

Chapter 9

The Day of Salvation

IT WAS NEW Year's Day, 1989, when I walked into a church called Faith Temple New Hope on Prospect Street in East Orange, New Jersey. The church had placed speakers on the outside of the building and I could hear the choir singing as I approached. The music captured me and before I knew it, I was inside the building, crying my heart out. The fact that I was crying also marked this as a very special day for me. I had not been able to cry for about two years. I remember at times trying to force myself to cry and I couldn't. I am not talking about shedding a few tears, I am talking about crying from my gut. I remember a couple of the ushers standing around, fanning me with those paper fans with the wooden handles. I felt sorry for them because I believed I was painful to watch.

The pastor of Faith Temple at the time was Milton Hobbs. He would become my first and one of the more impactful spiritual fathers I am blessed to have in my Christian journey here on earth. I am sure his message was powerful on that New Year's Day—they often were—but I just can't remember the message. All I can recall is hearing him make the call to come to salvation. I remember asking the ushers if I could go up, which of course they gladly led me down to the altar.

Confessing Jesus Christ as my Savior that day, I was born again. I was told that to be baptized was my next step. I was not sure what that meant, but I was on a roll in changing my life so I agreed to do it. The next thing I knew they gave me a pair of white pants and a T-shirt to change into. I was just flowing in the excitement of it all. At times, it appeared the church ministers and others were more excited than I was.

I remember there was a moment when the thought flashed in my head, *If they offer you something to drink, get the . . . out of here.* See, I did not know much about church, but I was familiar with Jim Jones. He was the cult leader under the guise of a pastor of a church, who gave his followers poisoned Kool-Aid to drink, killing all who drank it. I am so glad no one offered me anything to drink. I would have missed being placed into a giant metal tub filled with what had to be the coldest water on earth and slam dunked into it. I think coming up out of that water was the first time I consciously called on Jesus.

I had often wondered why my initial born-again experiences were not like many of the testimonies I would later hear. Like how people went down in the water hooked on drugs and came up delivered. That did not happen for me. As I think about it now, it may not have happened that way for me because that water was too cold for anybody to stay under. Their water must have been much warmer than mine. I did finally bury my old man, just not that day.

Pastor Hobbs invited (well, really he *told* me) to come to prayer on Tuesday night. I found a clean and safe place to sleep and keep my few belongings. Seton Hall University in South Orange, New Jersey, was building new student dorms. At night, I would slip through an opening in the fence and sleep inside one of the structures. I had managed to stay clean and was on my way to the church on Tuesday night.

While standing on the corner, two brothers I had sold drugs to and got high with pulled up. I had not seen these guys in years. They told me they had hit a house (robbed a drug house) and were going to get high and invited me to come. I knew that there was something extremely out of the ordinary. Without saying a word, I just took off running. For about three or more miles I ran a block and walked a blocked until I got to church. I know now that Satan was trying to keep me from making it to that prayer meeting on that night because that was the place and the night that God had commanded a blessing to be released for me.

I was used to praying. Growing up as a Muslim, I prayed five or more times a day. However, I was completely in the dark on praying as a born-again Christian. I was praying in the manner I was familiar with for a while. Then I just sat down and tears, once again, began flowing from my eyes. One of the mothers of the church came and sat down next to me. I told her my situation and she asked me what did I want from God. I answered her, "to be free from drugs." She told me that was something she knew God would be willing to give me. She then continued to explain what the word *hallelujah* meant. How it expressed the highest praise we can give God. She walked to the altar with me and began to pray. At first, I was just repeating or agreeing with what she was saying. Every now and then, I would throw in a "Hallelujah."

Soon all I was doing was praising God. I could not even hear her anymore. Then suddenly I was in a place in my mind that gave me a sense of peace I had never experienced before. I knew I was in the presence of God. I felt as if I was having a conversation with God, but I was not speaking English. This was an experience I never had before. I did not want this encounter with God to end, but I could feel my body getting weak. I had already dropped to my knees and could feel myself leaning forward. As my encounter ended and I became aware of my surroundings, I heard people screaming, praising, and shouting hallelujah all around me. I opened my eyes and saw people crying and hugging each other. I then realized I was completely soaked in my own sweat and tears. My body felt as if I was on fire.

The mother who was praying with me asked me to describe what had happened. In my attempt to explain, I mentioned that I was talking to God but I was not speaking English and everyone in to room began praising, shouting, and running around the room again. It was then explained to me what had taken place. I was filled with the Spirit of God with the evidence of speaking in tongues. I had no idea what "tongues" were. I had never even heard of tongues before. Everyone else seemed to be very happy I had it so it made me happy too. It would be some time later before I truly understood and realized the gift that God had given me that night. This experience also served as an anchor for me.

When some of my Muslim friends and family and street running buddies would attempt to discourage me from continuing with my decision to be a Christian, I had no words to respond with. However, what I did have and still have today is that experience of my first true encounter with God. In addition, I was determined to stay and see what else there was to this religion.

Chapter 10

I Just Wanted a Savior

THE NEW YEAR'S Day that I walked into Faith Temple Church and answered the call to salvation, I was not being honest with God, Pastor Hobbs, or myself. Granted, I did not fully understand at the time what was really going on within me. When Pastor Hobbs asked if I wanted to accept Jesus Christ as my Lord and Savior, I immediately replied "Yes!" The truth was that I was only seeking Jesus as a Savior, not Lord. I wanted Him to save me from the pain, guilt, shame, self-hatred, and other things that came with my addiction. As much of a mess as my life was in, I still was not willing to relinquish control of it.

For me, smoking crack served a purpose and fulfilled a need that nothing else could—the need to escape the person I had become and the life I lived. Nothing else afforded me the sense of peace, well-being, and pleasure that smoking cocaine did. It was not my drug of choice; it was my *only* choice. In addition, I enjoyed getting high. What I did not enjoy were the consequences that followed. To say I wanted and accepted Jesus as my Lord would have meant following and obeying

Him and not my addiction. My addiction was the one thing that was functioning in my life as both problem and solution.

For those who may not understand the difference, a savior is one who delivers or rescues. What is referred to as "called to salvation" in church services is really more of a question that a statement. The question is, Are you in need of rescue from any intolerable situation, bondage, hopelessness, or great danger from which you are unable to save yourself? The message of Good News is the message of salvation and the Savior. To accept someone or something as Lord is to declare that one possesses and exercises power and authority and to whom respect is therefore due. It is a title of dignity and honor, acknowledging the power and authority of the one it is applied to.

> The title "Lord," while not connoting divinity in the metaphysical sense, means that at his exaltation Jesus entered upon a new function as the representative of God's Lordship in the world and over the church (Phil. 2:11). It is henceforth through the exalted Jesus that God exercises Lordship or kingly rule. The two "Lords," God and Jesus, are distinguished from each other but not separated.

Not only did I lack understanding of this, having God as the "Master" of my life through Christ and the Holy Spirit was something I was not mentally ready for.

In truth, my thinking at the time was not that different from what many believers in the body of Christ (the church) think. That is, shaping and defining God, Jesus, the Holy Spirit, and the Scriptures to what fits us as opposed to being transformed by them. It is a concept that says we can function as molds that God can be poured into and take on our shape and function. This is much easier than our submitting ourselves to be placed on the potter's wheel to be shaped and molded.

Because of my one-sided acceptance of Jesus, my spiritual development as a believer was unbalanced and unfruitful. Therefore, I was not walking in victory or freedom. I was just a poster child of what could be. Actually, not what could be, but what is and just has not been accepted. I remained this poster child for several years.

Chapter 11

Marriage

I HAVE LEARNED that there are some very important elements in the cultivation of a godly marriage. They include the ability to believe, stand on, and have expectancy of the promises of God. Many of us treat the promises of God as cute, wise sayings to decorate our walls, cars, and refrigerators with. We can quote them, but we must advance beyond quoting to learning how to appropriate them. This starts with believing that God is faithful to His promises and will not let them return to Him void.

The fulfillment of God's promises will not always be according to what we want, or when we want it, but they are always kept. In light of this fact, there is something we must understand about the principles behind God's promises to us. The promises are given to us in two forms: conditional and unconditional. A conditional promise has a condition attached to it—we have something we must do in obedience before the promise is fulfilled. It is referred to as a "this for that." On the other hand, an unconditional promise is just the opposite. It is not dependent on any actions we need to take. Its power of fulfillment is strictly upon God.

The nature of God's promises is also two-fold. Some promises are personal and others are universal. The personal promise is strictly for one person at an appointed time. The universal promise has no limitations as to who can claim it and no set time limitation. One of the mistakes we make that weakens or destroys our faith is when we mistakenly or ignorantly make conditional and personal promises, unconditional and universal. If the promise is conditional, we cannot bargain with God about the conditions. God is not going to change them.

After the condition is met, sometimes we have to wait, and then we must exercise patience because the promise will only be fulfilled in God's timing. This lesson has become priceless to my wife, Bonita, and me because of the pain, tears, confusion, isolation, and hardship it cost us to receive it. It is a lesson that comes as a result of confessing and combining the revelation of God's will with our timing. This was one critical mistake Bonita and I made. We moved completely outside of the timing of God regarding our marriage.

We were married less than one year after I was saved. Our lives soon developed into a living hell. Bonita soon found that her life had been joined to another life that was in the middle of a vicious and deadly war with demonic forces of drug addiction. In the midst of what appeared to be a never-ending battle, we never stopped believing that we were meant to be together as husband and wife, but we moved according to our timing and not God's.

I had been off of drug use for several months. God restored my health and strength and supplied me with employment at Blue Cross and Blue Shield and housing. Things were looking up and on the outside I looked good. However, the outside did not tell the complete story of the inner warfare that was about to begin again. The Lord blessed me with a circle of new associates and friends that was soon to become my family; my wife was in that circle. I looked good on the outside, but I was still a man under construction and in much need of healing.

As a babe in Christ, I was completely unaware of what was going on at the time. Because of my painful existence and the pain I had caused to others, I put up a wall larger than the Great Wall of China. Bonita was the first woman in several years who managed to pull down a section of my wall big enough for her to step through and touch my heart with her compassion, concern, and prayers. In addition, she was the first person I wanted to trust. I was tired of not trusting anyone, not even myself.

Surely Bonita was my gift from God. But what I did not understand then was that she was the joy that was to be beyond my cross after I was delivered from my addiction. I stepped outside of God's timing and took my gift before the appointed time. In so doing, I found my gift and myself nailed to the cross of my affliction. On the surface, the waters were calm, but there was a powerful undercurrent of depression, anger, and drug addiction in my soul. I felt as if I were the only one on earth who was hurting and causing the pain and disappointment I did. How could anyone really understand how I felt? Who would even want to understand? The deeper parts of me were still in isolation.

Then there was my self-punishment. Here I served as investigator, prosecutor, judge, jury, and warden. I condemned any sign of happiness and joy in my life. I was self-sentenced to a life of self-inflicted pain without parole. This was my punishment for my selfishness, foolishness, and lustful living. My drug addiction served as both executioner and comforter.

I needed to be alone with God so that He could place me on the operating table and perform surgery before presenting my wife to me. He had given me a small peek at what He wanted to bless me with and I had no consideration of His timing.

I thank God that He blessed my wife with the strength, will, and grace to endure through my series of spiritual operations, of which she found herself a part. I guess on her part it was like visiting a friend in a hospital to encourage him or her, but finding herself snatched up, sedated, and placed on an operating table to provide blood transfusions, organ transplants, and skin grafts.

A part of me knew I was not ready to marry. I remember driving up to meet her parents (Pastor and First Lady) I told Bonita that if they told us we should wait, I would honor that. She agreed, but that didn't happen. Truth is I should have been man enough to slow things down. But my fear of the possibility of losing the one person I was able to share with without feeling judged, was a key factor. Another factor was my lack of understanding that I could go to God for myself. Having a relationship with God was still a concept I had not been able to take hold of. I have learned that there are two things a hellish marriage will make you do: pack up mentally or physically and leave or go to God in prayer like you never have before. Bonita and I had done both.

Chapter 12

Running from Myself

AFTER ACCEPTING JESUS into my life and hearing the many testimonies and lie-a-monies, my expectation was that I was free from the grip of my crack cocaine addiction. Very soon I was faced with the realization that reality does not always match up with expectation. The opportunity, drive, and desire to get high were still in my life and stronger than ever. I had confessed Jesus as my Savior and been water baptized, so according to my understanding those things should not have been happening. I eventually began using again.

One of the concepts of Alcoholics Anonymous is for individuals who are in recovery to make necessary changes in people, places, and things. Alcoholics Anonymous (AA) is an international mutual aid fellowship founded in 1935 by Bill Wilson and Dr. Bob Smith in Akron, Ohio. AA states that its primary purpose is "to stay sober and help other alcoholics achieve sobriety." This concept appeared to be the only thing I had not attempted in an effort to be free from my addiction. So my wife and I began making plans to move.

We narrowed our new location down to two cities, Denver, Colorado, and Atlanta, Georgia. My wife left the choice to me and I selection Atlanta. What helped make the decision to move to Atlanta was that my wife would be able to relocate through her job. We obtained some apartment books and selected an apartment complex close to my wife's job in Stone Mountain, Georgia. We packed the clothes we had and boarded a Greyhound bus to Atlanta.

Even on the day we left Newark, New Jersey, my addiction was in full combat mode. My father volunteered to take us to Penn Station to board the bus. He came by our apartment to pick us up, but I was not there. I was in the hallway of a nearby building smoking crack. By the grace of God, I had used all the crack I had and was able to summon up enough common sense and follow it in enough time to meet my wife and father and get to the bus just before it was about to leave.

The bus ride seemed to be the longest trip I had taken in my life. We must have stopped in every one-bike town between Newark and Atlanta. My emotions were all mixed up. Fear, anger, excitement, sadness, and relief filled my soul like a tossed salad. I knew I would miss home deeply, but I felt I had no choice.

I was not sure what to expect in Atlanta. It was March 1990. I remember it was evening when we got into the city. Since I was an urban baby, it brought me great joy to see the lit-up skyline of the city. It wasn't New York, but I would make it work. I began to get even more excited when we arrived at the apartment complex that we would now call our home. It was far above our expectations for the rental price compared to New Jersey/New York. The apartment felt like a house to us. The rooms were huge, we had a balcony, exercise room, swimming pool, small pond with geese (who knew I was from the north and chased me every day) and we even had grass and trees.

My wife's settlement into her new workplace seemed effortless. I soon landed a job with AT&T as a part-time telemarketer. With the grace of God on my life, I moved up quickly. Within three months, I was promoted to a full-time position. Three months after that I was promoted to supervisor of my group. The promotion came under some uncommon circumstances, along with the making of a few enemies, mainly those who were there much longer than I was.

It was funny to me that the circumstances through which I got my promotion were due to alcoholism. My supervisor at the time was battling with alcoholism. Due to my own background and the number of detox, treatment centers, and groups I had been through, it was easy for me to recognize. He was getting worse fast. He would leave for lunch and never come back. I started covering for him. One day I found him in his car passed out.

The next day I shared some of my story with him. Before I knew it, we were in his office crying and I prayed for him. Things did not change. I learned more and more about his duties and workload and did what I could. About a month later, he called a meeting and announced he was taking a leave of absence and I was being promoted to take his position. It took me completely by surprise. I remember racing home to share the news and celebrate with my wife. I remember thinking I had gotten my life back and all was fine.

I got another promotion, was making good money, building a career for myself, and my wife was about to have our first child. I had mixed feelings about that and I was not quite sure why they were so strong. Overall, things were going great with the exception of one thing. I was under the delusion that I could run from myself. Running from the people, places, and things was pointless because I had not dealt with me. I had not searched out the reasons within me why I turned to drugs as a coping tool and dealt with it. This underlying truth was why I had such strong mixed feelings about being a father.

What I failed to understand at the time was that I had run completely out of people and things to blame for my self-destructive lifestyle. The only thing left to blame was places. Being in New York/New Jersey was why I was still getting high. But now, in Atlanta, the harsh realities within myself still needed to be confronted. Running from place to place was not going to change that. Wherever I moved to, I was moving with me. The fear of examining who I had become just kept me going around in a vicious cycle of self-destructive behaviors and more problems than solutions.

The difference between self-condemnation and self-confrontation is important to understand. Self-confrontation is absolutely necessary. Self-condemnation involves knowing something against oneself by experience. Self-confrontation is necessary for growth. It is a "systematic attempt by an individual to understand his or her own personality without the aid of another person."[5] From my fruitless attempts to run from myself, I learned several truths. One is the fact that our personal history is being recorded every day and our past experience was once our future that we could have changed. The power of living in the "now" is the ability to shape, direct, and change our future. The direction this power takes is determined by the choices we make. Therefore, we must be careful not to allow our past to negatively determine the quality of our future. Instead we must use our past experiences to help us make quality decisions in the "now."

Self-confrontation brought me face-to-face with the fruit from the seeds that I had planted in my past. Negative and evil generational habits, thoughts and imaginations, beliefs, and principles were fruit growing within me. My harvest was the result of seeds of abuses, lessons learned in error or ignorance, and seeds planted by our environments and families.

In Paul's second letter to the church at Corinth, he shared something he had in his life that he referred to as a "thorn in his flesh," that God refused to take away from him. Paul came to this understanding as a result of self-reflection and confrontation.

We will not be healed, delivered, or restored until we are able to confront ourselves in truth and make a decision to move from where we are. The story of the prodigal son (which could also be called the extravagant or wasteful son), is an illustration of this truth.

> He wasted all his money on wild living. About the time his money ran out, a great famine swept over the land, and he began to starve. He persuaded a local farmer to hire him to feed his pigs. The boy became so hungry that even the pods he was feeding the pigs looked good to him. But no one gave him anything. When he finally came to his sense, he said to himself, "At home even the hired men have food enough to spare, and here I am, dying of hunger! I will go home to my father. . . ." (Luke 15:11-24)

After a series of bad choices and acting out of character, this son comes to his senses, returns to his father, confesses his sin, and is once against accepted as a son of the house. His first step was repentance, the realization of sin in his life. Then he came to repent as a result of his self-confrontation and took action by moving from where he was to where he wanted to be.

So we must be ready, willing, and able to confront, expose, and bring to God through prayer, our thorns of fear and false pride to obtain healing, deliverance, or grace to overcome their effects in our lives. Attempts to run from ourselves are a complete waste of time and energy.

Sometimes it takes trials, tribulations, and hardships to bring us to a point where we are sincerely ready for honest self-confrontation and openness to the will of God.

Chapter 13

The Ministry of Yakira

ON JUNE 24, 1991, my wife and I celebrated two major events: our second year of marriage and the birth of our firstborn daughter, Yakira. Before Yakira was even born, she was already declaring the wonders of God over man. Using the modern technology of the day, my wife's doctor informed us that our first child was a boy. The ultrasound picture seemed to confirm that.

On the day my wife gave birth, I stood right beside her witnessing the ugliness and beauty, the joy and pain of childbirth. As our child broke forth into this world, I realized that something was terribly wrong. A part of the anatomy that should be present on a male child was not there. Our firstborn was a girl.

Because we were expecting a boy, we had no name for her. She was known as "baby girl Reddick" for two days while I was at the library researching names. I presented my wife with several options and we settled on two Hebrew names, Yakira Rebecca. Yakira's language of origin is Hebrew and it is predominantly used in Hebrew. The name Yakira means "beloved, expensive, precious." Yakira is the feminine form of the Hebrew Yakar. Her middle name, Rebekah, is a Hebrew name. In Hebrew the meaning of the name Rebekah is captivating, knotted cord.

According to the 1991 U.S. Social Security Administration data, the name Yakira is not a popular baby girl's name in Georgia. Imagine that, only five babies in Georgia had the same name as she did in 1991. Across the entire United States, only twenty-seven babies also bore the same first name during the same year. From 1880 to 2013, the highest recorded use of the name Yakira was in 1997, with fifty-one babies.

Another aspect of Yakira that made her unique was her heart condition. She was born with congenital heart defects. The thing that made her heart condition so unusual was that each one of her defects served to lessen the problem caused by the other defects. According to the doctor who initially cared for her, Yakira should have been stillborn. However, God had other plans for her life.

Yet Bonita and I were still dealing with doctors telling us that our daughter would not live past eight months; Bonita being accused of not feeding and caring for our daughter; fighting with the hospital to release Yakira's medical records to Boston Children's Hospital for a second opinion.

Shortly after Yakira's records were delivered to BCH (Boston Children's Hospital), we were informed that she was in need of immediate open-heart surgery. We were told by medical personnel at the hospital in Atlanta that they would not be comfortable performing the procedure because Yakira was only three months old and severely underweight.

The surgeon at BCH who was willing and qualified to perform the surgery was leaving the country in four days. This meant we had three days to get Yakira to Boston. Initially this did not appear to be a big issue until Bonita and I discovered that we were not able to get a flight booked on any of the commercial airlines. Because of Yakira's heart condition, she required special oxygen equipment on the flight. None of the airlines was willing to take Yakira as a passenger because of this. So day one was spent being rejected by the airlines.

Day two was spent being rejected and directed down various rabbit holes by social agencies such as United Way, Red Cross, and others in our attempt to get assistance in getting our daughter to BCH.

During this period, Bonita, several members of the church we attended at that time, and I were praying and fasting. I felt as if my prayers were hitting the roof, so on day three I took a different approach. I must admit that what I did was not planned.

On day three, I went into work thinking there was no one else to call. At that time, I was working for AT&T as an account representative. I was just sitting at my desk that whole morning. There were so many thoughts running through my mind and I was beginning to feel overwhelmed.

During my lunch break I decided to go sit by a man-made pond behind the office building where I worked and pray. This prayer time was different. I was voiceless and motionless. I had run out of thoughts, questions, requests, breakthrough Scripture quotes, and demands. I was completely empty and alone.

After about forty-five minutes, I opened my mouth and simply said, "God, You chose Bonita and me to be stewards over Your child. She belongs to You. You led me to name her to reflect that she is Yours. For a moment I forgot that, so now I totally surrender her to You."

As I was about to get up and return to work, the Holy Spirit spoke to me and gave me these instructions: "Go upstairs, call AT&T headquarters, and tell them you need a jet." Yes, you read that right. That is exactly what I felt when I heard it. Yet I made the call. I would like to tell you that I made the call because I was so full of faith and power from God. The truth was that I made the call because I felt like a dying man who had nothing left to lose.

I placed the call to AT&T headquarters in Morristown, New Jersey, not far from the city where I grew up. I spoke with the manager of the aviation department. He patiently listened to me as I shared my situation with him. When I finished there was a long period of silence, then he responded with, "I am so sorry for you and your family, but there is absolutely nothing I can do."

I thanked him for taking the time to listen and hung up the phone. At this point, I was no longer speechless and empty. Now I was filled with anger to the point that it frightened me. I had the nerve to be angry with God.

It is now close to the end of my day at work. As I head back inside the building to my desk, I am thinking of the words to speak to my wife, expressing that I was unable to find a way to get our daughter to Boston in time. When I arrived at my desk, I found my manager there waiting for me. With tears in her eyes, she told me I needed to come with her.

We got on the elevator and proceeded to her manager's office. When we entered his office, he shook my hand and immediately starting dialing the phone. In my mind, I was thinking that this was about my daughter. Maybe she had passed and he was calling the hospital back.

He dialed what seemed to me a thousand numbers, said a few words, and handed me the phone. The voice at the other end of the phone greeted me and introduced himself as the vice president of Marketing. He told me the aviation department had shared my situation with him. He in turn shared my situation with his wife over lunch. Through her power of influence, she moved him to call. He continued to tell me that he was sending his company-assigned jet to Atlanta to pick my family and me up and fly us to Boston in the morning.

I believe I lost consciousness for a minute. I remember saying thank you, and after that the next thing I remember was being on my knees and praising God in tongues, other female co-workers were around me crying, male co-workers were shaking my hand but speechless. Then I realized I had to pull myself together to call my wife. I do not remember how I broke the news to her. I do remember her dropping the phone and doing what was most appropriate to do—praise God.

Bonita wanted to call to thank the vice president, but we could not reach him. So instead, she called two of the local news networks to tell them about the great deed AT&T had done for us. Within an hour and a half, Cynthia Goods, one of the local reporters was knocking on our door.

During our interview, Bonita was explaining Yakira's heart condition like a medical professional. During my interview, I was asked how did I feel about my company. All I could talk about was the goodness of God, most of which was not aired, but Yakira's story and picture were all over the news that evening, along with coverage in the Atlanta-Journal Constitution.

That morning when we arrived at the Peachtree Airport, news crews were waiting for us. I remember being interviewed by Kimberly Kennedy and she asked me what kind of work did I do for AT&T to make them willing to do this for me. My answer to her was that my position in the company was low level, but my position in the heart of God must be high. I recall getting the biggest smile and hug from her and at that moment the plane was landing.

When the doors opened we expected to see the pilot, but out walks the Vice President I had spoken to on the phone. He had flown down to meet us in person. While the reporters had him surrounded, Bonita and I boarded the jet and were completely amazed. It was like an apartment on wheels. Everything we needed for Yakira and more was on the jet. I was so excited and amazed that I kept telling myself to be cool, not to act like I had never been on a corporate jet before. However, I had not.

Once the jet was in the air, Bonita got her chance to personally thank him and I got the opportunity to share a little of my story with him. He was on his way to be dropped off in Washington, D.C., to meet with then President George Bush, Sr. He was serving on some kind of board regarding education. He asked me if I would mind sharing my educational experience with him. This discussion turned into my testimony. After spending what seemed like hours with him, we returned to the section of the plane where we were seated.

Bonita was sitting there crying. I said to her, "This is great, right?"

Her response to me was, "You don't see it, do you?" She reminded me that just a little over a year ago I was hooked on crack cocaine and homeless and I had just witnessed to one of the vice presidents of one of the most powerful companies in the world! Then I, too, started to weep.

When we arrived in Boston, there was an ambulance at the airport waiting for us. Somehow, the news networks in Boston had learned about the story and started airing it as well. As soon as we got to Boston Children's Hospital, they began examining Yakira to determine what surgery options would be available for her. It was explained to us that one of her issues was that she had two arteries connected to the same side of her heart, where one should have been connected on the other side of her heart.

One of the amazing things about Yakira's condition was that each problem with her heart helped lessen the negative effect of the other problem. For example, the "high side" of her heart where the two arteries were connected should have caused her heart to explode. However, on that same side of her heart was a hole, which allowed pressure to be released.

During our consultation with the surgeon, he presented us with what he thought would be the best option. It would mean that Yakira would not need to have as many surgeries in the future as her heart grew. He continued to explain that the best option that we all wanted was not available to us. It would have involved switching one of the arteries to the opposite side of her heart, and the artery was not long enough.

The morning of the surgery, I was granted permission to go into the room where Yakira would be and pray. I prayed over every individual, piece of equipment, and instrument I could think of and laid them all in God's hand.

About an hour before Yakira's surgery was to begin Bonita, her parents, and I were sitting in the family waiting room when her surgeon asked to see us. He took us into a room and showed us the X-ray of the artery we had seen the night before. He placed another X-ray image that was just taken on the screen. He circled both images where the arteries were and told us that the artery had grown several millimeters overnight. This cleared the way for us to have the procedure done that we all wanted. Again, we were all amazed by the grace and power of God.

Yakira had to be placed on an artificial heart-lung machine known as ECMO (extracorporeal membrane oxygenation). Traditionally, physicians have used ECMO to provide cardiopulmonary support to patients recovering from lung failure, heart failure, or surgery. Because of Yakira's age (three months) and weight, the plan was not to have her on the ECMO longer than ten hours. Anything above that raised the possibility of Yakira having brain damage.

A little over thirteen hours later, the surgery was completed without any issues except for the length of time. I remember Bonita and I hugging and thanking the surgeon for being there for our daughter. He appeared to be a little shaken. He shared with us how as a surgeon he saves lives almost every day. But this was the first time he could clearly say that it was all God's doing.

The next day, Bonita and I were scheduled to meet with a counselor to discuss how we would deal with Yakira having brain damage. However, that appointment was postponed because the EKG test on Yakira found no brain damage. She would have some light seizures, but that was it. Because of all that what was taking place with Yakira, she soon became the talk of the hospital. Nurses were asking to be placed with her, other parents who were there with their children were asking Bonita and me to come pray with them. Harvard Medical School asked our permission to use Yakira's condition as a case study, which we granted. Her speedy recovery was also the cause of much conversation among the staff and doctors.

By this time, I was starting to realize that Yakira was fulfilling the meaning of her name. She was being used as a "precious, priceless servant of God." Never had I been so proud of anyone before, as I was of her and being her father.

The following year my wife and I were blessed with twin sons, Malcolm and Mustafa. They were born July 15, 1992. Because they were born so close together in time, it was like having triplets.

Chapter 14

When I Caught Up with Myself

GOD HAD TRULY shown Himself to be real and active in my life. How could a person to whom God has been showing Himself stronger, make a decision to displease Him and themselves? I still ask myself that question.

A week after Yakira's operation, I had to return to Atlanta and get back to work. Bonita stayed with her parents in Boston so that Yakira could see her doctors at Boston Children's Hospital. My first day back at work I was greeted with bags of mail filled with greeting cards, cash, checks, and letters. The news stations had forwarded mail they received for Bonita and me.

I was feeling good about how things had turned out for Yakira and feeling good about myself. In my mind I was preparing to share these feelings and that's when it hit me—I was alone. This was the first time I had been alone after leaving Newark. The last thing I needed was to be alone with Kevin, who happens to be feeling good about himself.

I soon started questioning what right I had to be happy and proud of myself. I started thinking about my brother and how my niece and nephews are forced to grow up without their father. I thought about the various things I did against and to people; and I was alone. Who would know if I smoked away these tormenting thoughts?

One night cost me another five years in and out of my addiction. I left New Jersey in an attempt to run from myself, failing again to realize that wherever I went, I came along with me.

Falling back into my addiction meant falling out of accountability, responsibility, and control. In a short time, I lost my job, car, home, and the respect of my wife. The truth is I was only staying clean for my wife. It was not because I was delivered or obtained some high moral standard of living and self-control. She became my "No."

The problem was that no human being or any other creature should be considered my keeping power. That role belongs to God and the Holy Spirit alone. God has declared that there shall be no other gods before Him, which includes my wife.

The final event that caused me to lose my job at AT&T, which was also one of the most humiliating things I did in this season of my life, was borrowing money from a co-worker to cash my check and never returning it. It was as if I was operating on automatic pilot, driving directly to the crack house. I kept my co-worker's car the entire weekend. That Monday morning, I left the car in downtown Atlanta and had my wife call my co-worker to tell her where the car was. Little did I know that years later God would continue the humbling process through this act of mine.

My co-worker was (and still is today) a member of the New Birth Missionary Baptist Church, the church I would soon become a member of. I will never forget the deep shame I felt when I first saw her in church. When I finally got up the nerve to approach her and ask for her forgiveness, I was not expecting what I received. The compassion, love, concern, and joy of seeing me in church was unbelievable. Unfortunately, this would not be the last time I committed a crime against a church member. Again, I received sincere forgiveness, compassion, and concern.

And as the Bible states, the anguish I felt was as if they had dropped shovels of hot coals on my head.

So there I was, over 880 miles from New York/New Jersey, in Atlanta, Georgia, sitting in a crack house. It took a couple of years, but I finally caught up with myself, and the addiction followed with a vengeance. I spent another five years in homelessness, jail, and bondage before I caught a five-year prison sentence.

Chapter 15

Baldwin State Prison

WHILE SITTING IN a DeKalb County Jail cell waiting to be transferred to prison, I spent many days dreaming and thinking about a life of having no money concerns and traveling places teaching and preaching the Word of God. This became my coping device for getting through the day. While other inmates were watching TV (or arguing over it), playing cards, or on the phone, I would go to my cell, lie down, imagine, and dream. I began leading a small Bible study group in my dorm, which helped me.

As the days passed, tension began to build between myself and another inmate. I remember thinking how negative the situation was because he and I were the two oldest in the dorm. Instead of being positive role models in a negative situation, we were setting a bad example of using violence and intimidation.

I do not even know where the tension came from. I guess he was aiming to prove who was the alpha male between the two of us in the dorm. I had been in and out of jail several times and for the most part, been able to avoid physical confrontations, but I felt this was not going to be one of those times. My main concern was not having an additional charge placed on me, which might prolong my stay there. Therefore, I wrote a letter to the sheriff, requesting to have me moved to another dorm to avoid the confrontation I knew was coming.

After writing several requests, which had been ignored, one day during the lunch delivery to the dorm, what I was expecting happened. We got into a fight in which I smashed his face into one of the steel tables in the dorm. In doing so, I busted his bottom lip and nose, which required stitches. Also during our encounter, he bit me on my shoulder.

As soon as the officers came in and broke up the fight, I noticed that the skin was broken on my shoulder where I had been bitten. We both were taken to the infirmary where I requested that we both be administered an HIV/AIDS test. This request also was completely ignored. I continued to send letters expressing my concerns for thirty days. Then I was transferred to Baldwin State Prison to begin serving my five-year sentence.

Baldwin was a diagnostic prison where inmates came to be tested, evaluated, and assigned to one of the various prisons in Georgia based on the results of the diagnostic. Due to my test scores, education level, and legal background, I was assigned to stay at Baldwin. My detail assignment there was to work as a law library clerk. This was the best detail in the entire prison and doing something I loved to do, legal research.

This position also afforded me the opportunity to research, prepare, and file a lawsuit against the DeKalb County Sheriff and Jail for failure to intervene in a situation that caused me great emotional stress. I knew I had a case, but I was not sure I could prove it until I received my discovery request.

It sent me a mountain of paperwork. I think they forgot that I had nothing but time to read. In what I am convinced was a mistake, the officials included the letters and form requests I had sent to the sheriff. I kept reading them over and over because I thought it was just too good to be true. But it was, and it made my case.

After winning the summary judgment hearing, I knew it would just be a matter of time, and I had five years. After about three years, a team of attorneys for DeKalb County met with me to negotiate a settlement. I was more excited about winning the case than the money (but just for a moment). The settlement, along with money I was able to save during my work release at the halfway house, allowed me to go home to my family as a help, not a burden. This meant a great deal to me; it was the sweet part of this bitter experience.

The head librarian, Ms. Miller, was a Spirit-filled believer who immediately became a blessing in my life. After my thirty-day detail evaluation, I was permanently assigned to the position and was transferred from cell and dorm I was in to what was called the "Honor Dorm." This was where inmates who were placed on the honors list stayed. It was like moving from a Motel 6 to a five-star resort.

The building consisted of only four dorms; the inmates share a personal recreation area and two main rooms or common areas and were free to visit other dorms. Even our interaction with the officers was different, less confrontational. In addition, the head librarian introduced me to Chaplain Gayle and recommended me to be her assistant. So I also had the second best detail in the prison as a Chaplain's aide.

This position allowed me complete freedom throughout the prison campus. In all of this I was amazed at God's grace upon me. Both of these details allowed me to serve my time in a way that allowed me to feel that the time I was serving was not a complete waste of my time. I was soon overseeing the Christian services and Bible studies, counseling, and mentoring.

One of the most challenging and painful assignments I had was assisting inmates in applying for a program through Chapel Hill Harvester Church in Decatur, Georgia, that was sponsoring inmates for early release. The application process required the applicants to submit an essay explaining why they should be considered for the program and their plans should they be released.

I was writing essays for individuals; they would get accepted and be replaced. However, when I decided to apply for myself, I could not be accepted. At the time I was sentenced, the state had passed a law that required those who were found guilty of committing the crime I did to serve 90 percent of their sentence. Therefore, I was disqualified to participate in the program.

What was the most painful was witnessing guys being released from prison and in a very short period of time, returning back behind prison walls. I remember arguing with God about having to do this assignment. I was mad with God, the system, and myself. My one point of relief was helping a close associate of mine get accepted. Carlton was an exception. When he was released, he hit the ground running.

My other source of relief was being allowed to have my own Bible study. My Bible study was called "Video Empowerment." It was held very Wednesday evening in the library. In putting the study together, I contacted several ministries, requesting videos, reading materials, and tapes. Soon we were being flooded with teaching materials from around the country.

I remember sitting in the library with tears running down my face while reading a personal letter of encouragement from Dr. Myles Monroe of Nassau, Bahamas, along with boxes of material. I marked that as one of my life-impacting moments. I truly thank God for all the people and ministries who help the incarcerated.

There was one ministry that personally for me went above and beyond. My spiritual grandfather, Bishop T. D. Jakes, and The Potter's House, who not only provided tons of videos and material, but also allowed me to be part of their prison ministry, while I was in prison. I was blessed to be a contributing editor of their Prison Ministry newsletter that was circulated around the world.

Another life-impacting moment for me was reading letters forwarded to me from individuals around the world, sharing how my articles had blessed them, letters I still have to this day. Soon the editor of the newsletter and prison ministry directors George and Ruth Fitzgerald were mentoring me. It was out of this relationship that upon my release from prison I was blessed to briefly share a minute of my testimony with thousands of men during one of Bishop Jakes' conference in Atlanta, Georgia, called "Manpower."

Out of this I was blessed to share some of my testimony on Bishop Jakes' television show "The Potter's Touch." This airing was so impactful that it was re-aired several times in connection with a message by Bishop Jakes entitled "A Roadside Service." As great and exciting as all of this was, my connection with Bishop Jakes and The Potter's House had a far greater impact on my life.

It started as a normal day for me behind prison walls. I was called to report to Chaplain Jordan's office immediately. Upon my arrival there, she dialed a number and handed me the phone. On the other end of the phone was by mentor, Dr. M. C. Norman. He was the head deacon at New Birth Missionary Baptist Church, where my wife and I were members. He called to inform me that my eight-year-old daughter, Yakira, had transitioned.

She passed while at home with my wife, peacefully from heart failure. The last I remember Dr. Norman telling me was that our pastor, Bishop Eddie L. Long, wanted to make sure I knew that New Birth was taking care of all the homegoing arrangements and costs. After that, I seemed to have lost all consciousness. To this day I cannot recall what took place from the moment I hung up the phone until I became aware of being in isolation; I had been placed on suicide watch.

The level of pain and self-condemnation I felt was greater than what I experienced when my brother was murdered. I remember thinking what a horrible father and husband I was. Not being there for my daughter's last days and my wife having to deal with it as a single parent because I was incarcerated. What helped me survive the pain and despair was the outpouring of concern, compassion, support, and love from my pastor, my church, Mrs. Miller, Chaplain Jordan, my counselor, and even my fellow inmates.

I fully realized it when I was called to the warden's office. He needed to speak to me in reference to attending my daughter's homegoing service. Everyone mentioned above were working together to get me a pass to attend her service. New Birth was even willing to pay the cost of my security detail. The Department of Corrections refused to grant me permission, basically because of my criminal history and the circumstances.

The warden called me to his office to personally share his regret and explain to me why I would not be able to attend. I could feel his sincere regret and was honored that he thought enough of the situation and me. Normally, the chaplain or counselor would have handled this. What touched me the most was when I learned that my chaplain, on her personal time, drove from south Georgia to Atlanta to attend my daughter's service.

In addition to this, my friend Carlton, whom I had helped get released, also drove four hours with his small son to show respect to my daughter. He introduced himself to my wife and told her he "had to be there to represent me." I will never, ever forget that.

During this time of pain and once again questioning God's love for me, The Potter's House sent a DVD series of messages from Bishop Jakes entitled "The Church on Fire." In this series was a message entitled "The Day the Teacher Went Back to School." In this message Bishop Jakes taught about how God loves us so much that He clothed Himself in human flesh to understand what I was going through. I kept listening to that message over and over again until it filled my heart that in spite of my wrongs, shortcomings, and sin, God still loves me.

It was then that Jesus was elevated in my life from just being my Savior to being my Lord as well. It was then that I determined in my heart that I would be a better man for God, my wife, my daughter, and myself, by serving God in any way I can.

I was so focused on God, serving, and building my relationship with Him that I was no longer counting days, weeks, and months. God continued demonstrating His love for me through individuals. He moved in the hearts of my counselor, Ms. Miller, Chaplain Jordan, and the Warden to recommend and approve me to enter a work release program. I had no idea they had done so.

One morning I was awakened at 3:00 a.m. and told to pack up my things because I was being transferred. They would not tell any of us where we were going for security reasons. I will never forget waking up on the bus and seeing the Atlanta, Georgia, skyline. I knew then that wherever I was going, it was going to be closer to family. I had been transferred to the Atlanta Transitional Center. No barbed wire fences, bars, guard towers, or cells. The place looked like a well-kept townhouse in the heart of Atlanta. My first night was spent glued to the window, looking at cars and buses go by, people walking the street, and the skyline. After three and a half years I could taste that my freedom was near and that God is good.

Chapter 16

Back to the World

BEING AT THE Atlanta Transitional Center was like being back in the land of the living. I continued serving God as the chaplain's aide and was initially assigned a work detail in the kitchen. I quickly settled myself in and completed all of my classes and other requirements. As time approached the approval of my first visit, I felt like a kid on Christmas Eve. I couldn't sleep the night before and the day of visitation and every time the intercom would come on, my heart would stop, waiting to hear my name.

Visitations were completely different from those in prison. Family and friends were allowed to bring in newly purchased items from the store and there were board games, cards, etc., we could use with our visitors. For my wife and sons to come and see me in regular clothes and be able to interact with me was a gift from God.

Just like at Baldwin State Prison, I kept myself busy. The chaplain entrusted me to do a lot, including managing the Sunday services and Bible study. I started a video ministry, as I had done in the library at Baldwin, at the Transitional Center. The warden, Mr. Arrington, gave me permission to turn a large utility closet into a Christian library.

I conducted another letter writing campaign to various churches. I received a bigger response than when I did it at Baldwin. We even got a television and VCR players (for the younger readers, this was like a disc player that used tape). We built shelves, refurnished some old furniture, painted, and decorated as if we were building a temple for God. At the "grand opening" the warden, staff, and residents (as we were now called) could not believe it. That was one of my proudest moments in a long time.

On Friday and Sunday nights we would show Christian or inspirational movies. Thursday nights were Video Ministry and on Monday, Wednesday, and Friday we were open to check out books or tapes. Sometimes staff members would come and participate in our discussions after the videos. After every session I led, I would always advise the men not to let the smell and taste of freedom lead us to make a bad decision that could keep us from having that freedom. Little did I know at the time that the very thing would happen to me.

At the Transitional Center, privileges were earned. Outside work details, outside jobs, home visits, and even store visits were privileges we had based on our security clearance and our behavior. I remember that after my first home visit I was angry because my wife got me back to the center about twenty minutes early. She was going to make sure I got back on time so I could get another home visit. My goal was to earn an overnight. Those were hard to get.

When I was qualified for outside work release, I felt a great sense of pride just to be able to go out and look for a job. My focus was on restaurants because in my inside and outside work detail I served as a cook. In fact, I worked in the Georgia State building that housed many of the state agencies, including the Department of Corrections and the Pardon and Parole Board. I worked breakfast and lunch shifts as well as special events at the building or the governor's house.

One day, on returning to the Center from an interview, I walked passed Publix supermarket. I walked everywhere I could. I preferred to walk as opposed to catching a bus if I could. I had enough time to go in and complete an application. I also visited each department in the store, asking if they were hiring. I was blessed at the deli department. They were looking for help and I was able to speak with the deli manager, who happened to be from the "hood" in Brooklyn. I told her my story and situation. She was like "Okay cool, I'll call you."

When I got to the Center, the restaurant I had interviewed with called my counselor offering me the job. As soon as I started to rejoice, the Spirit of God said, "This is not the job for you. Wait for Publix." The problem with that was that residents were not allowed to turn down a job. One could be sent back to prison for doing so. I had no idea if or when Publix would call. And even if they did, it would be for a second interview.

I did not sleep all that night. I kept reminding God of the situation I was in, as if He did not know. The following day, I did all I could to avoid my counselor. It worked but he left word that he needed to see me the following day. This meant I was put on hold from leaving the building at all.

When I met with him I explained my position as best I could that would make sense to him and I put it all on God. My hopes were that mentioning "God" would scare him a little. But no such luck. The funny thing was, I was sitting there telling God to tell him what He told me. God's grace did prevail and I was given twenty-four hours to accept the job or go back to prison.

About two hours after leaving him, I was called back to his office. I got there and he told me Publix had called and wanted me to come in for a second interview. Now my counselor was dealing with me as if he was afraid of me. I felt like the little kid who was being bullied and picked on until his big older brother shows up.

I got my pass, ran to my room to change clothes, and headed to Publix, which was only about four blocks away. When I arrived I had my best interview face on. I had already rehearsed answers to questions I thought they might ask. Once I was seated in the deli manager's office, she asked me a few questions about the center and then concluded with "When can you start?" and "Can you work full time?"

My answers were "today" and "absolutely." I would later learn about the great benefits I had for my family and me. I also learned that almost everyone who works retail at Publix supermarket starts part-time. But God . . .

The greatest blessing of being at the transitional center was being able to work and save money. I did not want to return to my family as a burden financially. I was able to save a great amount of money for someone coming out of prison. I was getting a lot of overtime at work because I was always willing and able. In addition, I had received my settlement from my lawsuit against DeKalb County Jail.

Although the Center allowed us to send money home, it was not much. I needed to help my wife out a little more. She was struggling with two children. I decided when I received my settlement that I would use that to open a bank account. Because there was a Washington Mutual bank just a few feet from my job and the manager was a customer of mine at Publix, I was able to do so.

Having the account really made me feel good. The problem was that residents were not allowed to have outside bank accounts. So I had to hide the fact that I had one. Therefore, I would give my wife any receipts or paperwork I had along with the cash and leave my ATM card in my locker at work. Things were working out great.

One day my wife came by the store to pick up some money and I forgot to give her the receipt. It was still in my wallet. When I was checking into the center, I was searched and the officer found the bank receipt. The following day I told the warden the complete truth. It was considered a major violation and I was sent back to prison.

Even in this bad situation, God was still blessing me. The warden was a fair and very decent man. In my experience he was a rare find. He helped arrange for me to go to a private prison. It was much more relaxed compared to Baldwin. It was located in south Georgia, about two and a half hours from Atlanta, so I told my wife not to visit. At that point I only had six months left on my sentence. Because of God's grace and my work ethic, Publix hired me back upon my release and I have been with the company since then.

Chapter 17

Answering the Call

UPON MY RELEASE from prison, I had two driving desires: keep the promises I had made to God and take care of my family. I first had to determine if I was going to stay in Atlanta or move to Dallas, Texas. I was strongly leaning towards moving to Dallas and joining T. D. Jakes' ministry. I had already made connections and served as part of their prison ministry.

To be honest, my strongest motivation was shame and guilt. I had hurt some people very close to me and I was embarrassed to return to New Birth. This was the church I was attending prior to being incarcerated. But I could not overlook all that New Birth had done for my family and me while I was incarcerated. With all of these thoughts swimming in my head, I resolved them all when I remembered my promise to God and God was not releasing me from New Birth.

So in keeping my promise I returned to New Birth. This is also when I settled in my mind that God has a sense of humor. When it was settled that I would be staying at New Birth, I asked God where I was to serve. The answer I received was Prison Ministry. Though it may appear to be an obvious choice, it was not mine. I was ready to forget prison and all that came with it. However, more importantly, the director of the prison ministry and I were not on the best of terms before my incarceration. He was done with me and rightly so. I was hell on two feet. Yet God told me to serve him with honor and respect.

When I approached him and told him what God had said, I received a welcome that I was not expecting. After a few months passed, he apologized and ask me to forgive him because he was wrong. I was so blown away. I was the one going around asking for forgiveness. God moved in that situation and we developed a great working and personal relationship that continues to this day.

Things were moving and happening so quickly I really did not have time to think about adjusting to being free; I just had to make the adjustments and lean on God. About two months after my release, I was invited to share my testimony at a T. D. Jakes men's convention, Manpower, in Atlanta, Georgia.

I will never forget that evening. I remember standing on the same stage, at the Georgia Dome, as my spiritual grandfather (Bishop T. D. Jakes). I did not know that my spiritual father (Bishop Eddie L. Long) was the speaker that evening. Looking at what looked like a sea and mountains of men in front of me and several great men of God I admired behind, I thought, *Kevin you are way out of your league.* My heart was beating so fast and hard I just knew everyone else could hear it.

Then a peace came over me and I heard these words, "Just tell My story." Then I understood that my life was (and still is) used as a pen to write the story of His love, grace, and power. My testimony is His story.

Following that evening, I was blessed to share my story on T. D. Jakes' television program "The Potter's Touch." Then that segment was added to a message Bishop Jakes preached entitled "Roadside Service." That message, along with several rebroadcasts of The Potter's Touch show, allowed my pain and tears to be a blessing and encouragement to thousands around the world. Only a great and loving God would do such a thing.

One of the prayers I prayed often, and I do so even to this day, was not to be a public success, but a private failure. My failure I am referring to is giving up. I knew working on my marriage and seeing that my wife got the time, healing, and breakthrough she needed would be challenging.

In every marriage, there are seasons, circumstances, trials, tribulations, hardships, challenges, strongholds, and traditions that confront and attack it. In dealing with these attacks, King Solomon suggested that we seek wise counsel. "And a man of understanding will attain wise counsel" (Prov. 1:5).

Jesus taught us to pray to the Father about the attacks from the enemy. But He also taught an important lesson that many of us fail to apply habitually, and that lesson was to speak the Word over such attacks. Often we spend too much time speaking about our problems. Jesus told us to speak *to* our problems. "So Jesus said to them, 'Because of your unbelief; for assuredly, I say to you, if you have faith as a mustard seed, you will say to this mountain, 'Move from here to there,' and it will move; and nothing will be impossible for you" (Matt. 17:20).

Jesus also gave us an example when He was under attack by Satan in the wilderness. He did not pray or seek counsel. Sometimes we will not have time to do either of those things. We will only have time to do what Jesus did. He simply spoke the Word. In other words, what Jesus needed to overcome the attack was already in Him. The same is true for us. Our key to victory against every attack that comes against our marriages is already within us.

Too often we look for solutions from outside sources to come in and make the change and provide the victory. But victory and change with God comes as a result of processing from the inside out. That is why one writer stated that we are to work out our own salvation. Deliverance, salvation, healing, authority, and power are within us, insured by the Holy Spirit. We just need to start working it out.

> In addition, I realized that for my wife and me, being religious would not be much help. Then Paul stood in the midst of the Areopagus and said, "Men of Athens, I perceive that in all things you are very religious, for as I was passing through and considering the objects of your worship, I even found an altar with this inscription: TO THE UNKNOWN GOD. Therefore, the One whom you worship without knowing, Him I proclaim to you. (Acts 17:22–23)

A major error in thinking that has infested the church and marriage is that concerning religion. According to Webster's Dictionary, religion is defined as "a personal set or institutionalized system of religious attitudes, beliefs, and practices; scrupulous conformity." Although religion acknowledges the existence of God (which demons also acknowledge), many of the individuals consumed within it are ignorant of Him. Because they have no relationship with Him, they fail to enter into the lifelong and rewarding process of knowing Him. To them He too is really an "unknown God." As a result, many have confused being religious with being relational and spiritual. They confuse acts and practices with relationship and condition. They also make the mistake of believing that being religious would be enough to sustain their marriages.

In his youth, King David defeated a great warrior and became a mighty man of war because of his confidence in God. His confidence was a result of his knowledge and understanding of God. David stood on his personal experiences with God, not on a religious system. You may be able to religiously worship an unknown god, but you will never be able to enter into a completely trusting relationship with him. How can you truly trust in him whom you do not know? How can you completely trust in a spouse who says that he or she is being led by a god unknown to you and even to your spouse?

In fact, we can only give as much of ourselves as we know and understand to as much of God that we come to know and understand. I could not walk in the victory of being free from the fear of being homeless and hungry again without knowing and understanding my self-reliance needed to be destroyed. I could not trust God with these issues without knowing and understanding His character as the One who foresees and provides, heals and delivers.

This operation of religion in our lives creates a desire in us to give an outward religious performance, be it preaching, teaching, serving, etc., but we never really face some of the deep and ugly things going on inside of us. It is these things that have been eating away at our marriages.

So while I was incarcerated and had the time, I studied everything I could find about marriage and being a man in the Scriptures. When I was released, I had two large three-ring binders filled with notes. At times I would share from those notes while serving. One day I was sharing with some evangelism team members and one of the young ladies commented "You've got enough notes for a book."

A few weeks later, another young lady came to me and told me that God had laid it on her heart to edit my notes into book format. About a year later, my first book was published, *Marriage According to the Kingdom.*

My family and I moved from the apartment my wife had been living in because that apartment was too small. We found a decent bigger apartment that I was able to afford and was approved for. We had been living there for about one and a half years when I got a notice that we had ninety days to move out because of my criminal background. The owners had decided to conduct background checks on current residents and applicants.

We were wasting a lot of money on applications and dealing with a lot of rejection applying to apartment complexes, which were all doing background checks. I was switching my plans now to just fight them in court.

About six weeks before our court date, I started my backup plan to start applying with homeowners looking to rent. In asking around we were introduced to a real estate couple who also attended New Birth. They said they could help us get into a house. I didn't think my credit would be good enough, but God knew. In exactly six weeks we were moving into our newly built home.

The more I grew in God, the more He showed me parts of my assignment. Soon it became clear that I was to be an interruption in my bloodline. One of those assignments was to earn a college degree. No male in my immediate bloodline had been able to complete that accomplishment.

I began in 1977 at Kean University in Union, New Jersey. After two years I transferred to Rutger's University in Newark, New Jersey. But I did not finish my degree program.

Therefore, I enrolled at Beulah Heights University. While a student, I still was serving at church and working a fifty-hour week. What helped me get through was remembering that it wasn't just about me. With the grace of God, I have earned an Associate's Degree in Biblical Education and Bachelor's and Master's Degrees in Religious Studies.

I am currently serving as an elder/teacher at New Birth, developing a ministry for men called Manhood 712, and preparing to start classes toward my doctorate. I have learned from many, many lessons in my life. One vitally important lesson I have learned is that there are times in my relationship with the Lord when His answer or response is not as important as His acknowledgment that He heard me. This lets me know that our lines of communication are still open. He is paying attention to me and can hear my cry.

Regardless of how strong one's faith may be, there are times that love needs to be confirmed. This can be accomplished by the simple act of receiving, paying attention to, and actively listening to what another has to say and expressing that we have done so. The word *now* is a confirming word. It refers to "the present time or moment." The love Jesus had for Martha, Mary, and Lazarus was confirmed before and after He received the news that Lazarus was sick.

However, when confirmation is not followed by demonstration, questions arise. What kind of love is this? In dealing with this question we must first understand that

life circumstances are not indicators of God's love for us. They provide avenues through which His love flows, but they are not the determining factors.

God's love for His own is not a pampering love; it is a perfecting love. The fact that He loves us, and we love Him is no guarantee that we will be sheltered from the problems and pains of life.

I have just shared with you some of the issues I had to overcome and grow from. I know that many of these issues are not assigned exclusively to me. Many of you have faced or are facing some of the same demons. I remember the moment shortly after I was able to exhale, when I began piecing together all of the various components of my life. I resolved to ask God one question, Why did I have so many issues? Like the issues in my life, the answer was not exclusively mine.

So in conclusion, I would like to share the revelation that was given me in hopes that it may help other men to accept and understand the reasons for the issues in their lives.

We must never think that love and suffering are incompatible. Because Lazarus was targeted by God, his life was destined to bring glory to God. There is no longer any doubt in my mind that, like Lazarus, I am the target of God's love. Therefore, my life is also destined to bring glory to God.

Endnotes

1. Philadelphia Tribune, July 2, 1963, p. 3.

2. Malcolm X, "End of White World Supremacy," p. 25; *Playboy* interview, p. 62.

3. *Martin and Malcolm and America, A Dream or a Nightmare*, James H. Cone, ©1991, Orbis Books, p. 194.

4. Paul J. Achtemeier, Harper & Row and Society of Biblical Literature, *Harper's Bible Dictionary* (San Francisco: Harper & Row, 1985), p. 573.

5. *Merriam-Webster's Collegiate Dictionary*, (Springfield, MA: Merriam-Webster, Inc., 2003).

Contact Information

To order additional copies of this book, please visit
www.redemption-press.com.
Also available on Amazon.com and BarnesandNoble.com
Or by calling toll free 1-844-2REDEEM.

CPSIA information can be obtained
at www.ICGtesting.com
Printed in the USA
FFOW05n0932240517

9 781683 143130